Things the Manual
Never Told You
IBM PC Edition

THINGS
THE MANUAL
NEVER TOLD YOU
IBM PC Edition

Tips, Techniques, and Shortcuts from the Nation's Largest User Group

Compiled by
The Boston Computer Society

Edited by Jack McGrath

Addison-Wesley Publishing Company, Inc.
Reading, Massachusetts   Menlo Park, California   New York
Don Mills, Ontario   Wokingham, England   Amsterdam
Bonn   Sydney   Singapore   Tokyo   Madrid   Bogotá
Santiago   San Juan

The System Board Component Diagram on p. 10 is reprinted by permission from the IBM PC Technical Reference Manual, © 1983 by International Business Machines Corporation.

The Impact and Nonimpact Printer diagram on p. 36 is reprinted from *PC* Magazine, November 27, 1984 © 1984 Ziff-Davis Publishing Company.

Library of Congress Cataloging-in-Publication Data

Main entry under title:
Things the Manual Never Told You.

Includes index.
1. IBM Personal Computer.   I. McGrath, Jack.
II. Boston Computer Society.
QA76.8.I2594T55   1985   001.64   85–11160
ISBN 0–201–10706–6

Cover design by Marshall Henrichs
Set in 11-point Century Schoolbook by Donnelley/ROCAPPI, Inc., Cherry Hill, NJ
Text illustrations by Barbara Frake

EFGHIJ–DO–8987
Fifth Printing, June 1987

Contents

Tips Topics

The Boston Computer Society (BCS) had humble beginnings. Its first meeting, in February 1977, took place in the library of a small high school in Boston. Two people showed up. (One of them had been working late at the school and wandered in by accident.)

Our first month, however, established a precedent for the future of the BCS and for personal computing in general. We experienced *explosive* growth: in one month, meeting attendance soared by 300 percent.

Six people showed up.

Personal computers were a new idea at the time. In fact, many users shunned the term *personal computer;* they preferred to call their systems *microcomputers* to differentiate their microprocessor technology from mini and mainframe computer systems. Most of these adventurous pioneers were extremely knowledgeable in the areas of electronics, computer design, and software. A strong technical background was an absolute necessity for computer ownership, because most microcomputers in early 1977 were sold in kit form and required thousands of solder connections and dozens of tests to assemble. Getting a computer to *work* was a formidable challenge; doing anything useful with it sometimes seemed impossible.

Sparked by a lack of information or support for users, microcomputer clubs and societies started to form throughout the United States in 1975. They provided an important forum where users could exchange technical information and learn from one another's experiences.

From its inception, the BCS was different. Although we offered a place for technical users to exchange ideas, the BCS was never driven by a desire to create a club for technocrats. Instead, we wanted to demystify computers and provide a means for *anyone* to feel comfortable with the technology and to learn about its practical applications.

Foreword

Jonathan Rotenberg
President
The Boston Computer
Society

In the early days, this didn't always work. Although we became fairly aggressive about publicizing the BCS's fledgling monthly meetings in local newspapers and calendar iistings, new attendees were often bewildered by the technical language that permeated meetings. Furthermore, many of our regular attendees—who were very technically sophisticated—didn't necessarily agree with the BCS's outreach mission; they wanted a small club in which they could talk shop with one another in their native tongue of computer jargon.

It wasn't even clear that the BCS was a viable idea. I remember speaking with one of the leading microcomputer designers of the time, who told me that "there's no future for this technology with consumers. Microcomputers will never be useful to anyone except electronics hackers."

In late 1977, however, the industry introduced a new generation of computers. Suddenly, the BCS made sense. The new systems—the Apple II, Commodore PET, and Radio Shack TRS-80—were a radical departure from the past, because they were small, fully assembled, relatively inexpensive, and easy to use. Some people called them *appliance computers* because you could buy and use them as you would an appliance. Although there was little practical software available for these systems, the user no longer had to have a degree in engineering to operate them. For the first time, a 110-volt outlet and the touch of a power switch were all that was required to have a functioning computer.

The appliance computer had a profound impact on the BCS. Attendance at our monthly meetings had been averaging 20 to 30 people. On the night we presented the new TRS-80 Model 1, close to 90 people jammed into our tiny meeting room. (We later discovered that nearly half of the attendees were Radio Shack salespeople who had come hoping that the BCS would demystify this portentous new addition to their stores.)

It was the dawn of the personal computer as a mass-merchandised product. Over the coming years, millions of nontechnical people would become interested in computers, hoping to save themselves time, improve their work efficiency, make their homes more interesting, and enrich their lives. Most would face a rude surprise: buying and owning a personal computer isn't as simple as the ads would have you believe.

As useful software and practical support products became available, more people could rationalize climbing on the personal-computer bandwagon. But the more they tried to accomplish specific tasks with their computers—automating their companies' accounting, getting printers to run with their PCs, or organizing filing systems, for example—the more they discovered how difficult it was to get help. There were consultants, but few users could justify spending more for a consultant than for their entire system. There were computer salespeople, but most were more interested in *selling* computers than in helping customers. There were also dozens of magazines, but they were highly technical and could never provide the kind of moral and personal support that users needed so desperately.

Thus, the BCS began to evolve to address the support and education needs of a new generation of computer consumers. Following a successful public computer show we ran in 1978, we started a newsletter for our members called *The BCS Update*. Like the BCS, the *Update* began humbly. The first issue was one page and was typed on a cheap typewriter. Also like the BCS, however, it grew rapidly.

One of the most important things to happen to the *Update* took place in December 1978. We were looking for a member to volunteer to become editor of the *Update,* and at our December meeting a man named Fred Guidry stepped forward. Fred, it turned out, was the arts and entertainment editor of *The Christian Science Monitor.* He had never seen a computer magazine and didn't realize that computer publications were supposed to be inscrutable, clumsy-looking, and written in "computerese." All he knew was how to produce witty, concise, effervescent writing.

Within two years, the newsletter metamorphosed into *Computer Update,* a full-color, nationally distributed glossy magazine. The *Update* is still unique in its in-depth coverage of the personal computer world and its hard-hitting, consumer-oriented reporting and provocative commentary.

In 1979, we started our first user group. Realizing that many of our members now owned personal computers and were finding it difficult to get the specific information they needed at our general meetings, we created these groups to provide special support for each brand of personal computer.

By 1981, we were starting new user groups at a furious pace. Most grew into entire organizations within the BCS, providing meetings, workshops, newsletters, publications, software libraries, subgroups, satellite groups, electronic bulletin boards, and telephone assistance. Unfortunately, a number of groups eventually watched their systems become casualties of industry shakeout when personal computing entered a new chapter: Chapter 11. (Even for "computer orphans," however, the BCS today continues to be a source of inspiration and support.)

As more of our members became focused on what they wanted to accomplish with their computer, rather than on the specific model they owned, the BCS started special-interest groups. These were like user groups except that they were organized around computer applications, such as education, business, law, real estate, nonprofit/public sector, and publishing. We also started groups for interests such as graphics, artifical intelligence, networks, social impact, telecommunications, and robotics. (We even started a group called Family HUG—the Family Home User Group.)

Today the BCS has 44 user and interest groups covering virtually every aspect of personal computers. In addition, we have started a member-discount program, a computer-resource center, a variety of on-line information systems, and several dozen other services. Membership is nearly 20,000, with members throughout the United States and in 20 other countries.

It's difficult to explain exactly what the BCS has turned into, because analogies are not readily available. In 1982, the *Boston Phoenix* wrote, "The BCS fills the gap left by an industry that grew faster than its ability to explain itself." *Tech Weekly* said, "The BCS may turn into the American Automobile Association of the 21st century." Some of our members have even said they think of the BCS as "the PBS of the computer world."

Despite the dramatic coming of age of personal computers and the BCS, I think that little has really changed in the personal computer world since the appliance computers of 1977 were unveiled. In general, personal computers have become more powerful and easier to use. The software has become more versatile and can handle ever more complex applications. However, although users are probably accomplishing a lot more with their personal computers now, they seem to have as many frustrations and problems today as they did in 1977.

I remember an interesting conversation I once had with Steve Jobs, then chairman of Apple Computer.

"What does the BCS do?" he asked.

I explained.

"That's very interesting," he said. "But you know, organizations like the BCS aren't going to be around for much longer."

"Why is that?" I asked.

"Because we're going to make personal computers as easy to use as Xerox machines. There's no such thing as a user group for Xerox machines, and it would be ridiculous to have one."

Feeling a little alarmed by this death proclamation for the BCS, I wondered if he was right about the future of personal computers. It was true that personal computers would become much easier to use and would require less training to operate.

There is, however, an important difference between a personal computer and a Xerox machine. The latter does just one thing: it makes copies. It might reduce them or enlarge them or collate them, but it still has one simple purpose.

In contrast, consider the simplest, easiest-to-use spreadsheet program available for PCs. There is no easy way to explain what it does. Moreover, the kinds of applications for which people use spreadsheets—budgeting, financial projections, etc.—can be elaborate. Combining a complicated application with a complicated technology tends to be far more complex than the sum of the parts.

There's also the fact that when you remove a spreadsheet disk from a computer and put, say, a data base program in its place, you suddenly have a totally different machine with new challenges and problems.

But I think there's an even more ominous difference between the personal computer and the Xerox machine. When a Xerox machine breaks, the worst that can happen is that you have to take your copying work elsewhere. When a personal computer breaks, however, you can lose forever invaluable, irreplaceable information. The more information you trust to a personal computer, the more you can lose.

Until the personal computer industry crosses the frontiers of artificial intelligence and designs machines that can take care of themselves, that are equipped for virtually any application, and that can figure out what their users want them to accomplish, I think the BCS will have an ever-increasing role in the lives of personal computer users, consumers, and the general public.

For the present, the BCS is still growing and changing. Besides adding new services for our members and expanding current services, the BCS is reaching out in new directions.

We're finally beginning to realize many of our founding ideals and are bringing computer education and demystification to ever-broadening audiences. Beyond serving our members, we feel that the BCS—as the nation's largest non-profit computer association—can be an influential voice for all consumers, and we're playing an increasingly active role in consumer advocacy issues.

We're also deeply concerned about larger social issues surrounding the proliferation of personal computers. We've seen a strong tendency for computers to contribute to the widening gap between the "haves" and "have-nots" of the world and to leave the disenfranchised of our society in worse shape than ever. To address this problem, the BCS is working with neighborhood groups, school systems, industry, and many of our members to start grassroots, neighborhood-based computer-access programs.

Another concern regards the impact of computers on the quality of our lives. We've seen the negative, desocializing effects computers can have on kids, and we fear that computers will have a more destructive impact on people's relationships—both at home and at work—than they may realize today. We're working with The Computer Museum in Boston to develop interactive exhibits that will delve into these issues and cause people to think about the positive and negative aspects of the information revolution.

As far as our mission to help personal computer users get the most out of their systems is concerned, we've begun to reach out beyond our membership and provide service to nonmembers. In fact, this book is the first example of such a service.

We've tried to capture a lot of the helping and information exchange that happens in our member services within the pages of this book. Like all BCS services, the book has come about through the hard work of a lot of devoted volunteers.

Many people deserve recognition for their work on this book. First and foremost is Jack McGrath. As editor/writer, he took on a massive task of compilation and coordination, and wound up doing much more writing than we originally anticipated. Terry Catchpole coordinated the book from The Boston Computer Society side, and, by his good business and editorial sense, made the procedure much smoother than it would otherwise have been.

For initiating the entire project, thank you to Jim Hassett (Addison-Wesley) and Ted Ricks (BCS). At Addison-Wesley thanks are also due to Editor-in-Chief David Miller who supervised the project, editor Ted Buswick who worked closely with Jack McGrath and helped determine the book's format, and Beverly

Thomas who supervised the book through production.

The following people either completed questionnaires or offered sound suggestions while this book was in progress. The BCS thanks them all for contributing the numbered tips that you'll find in the book. Thanks go to: Martin Agulnek, Ramon Alonzo, Berberian & Associates, Jessica Berman, Carl Binder, William Bixby, Steve Blake, John Bliss, Cliff Brown, Douglas Carnahan, George Cookman, Gerald Craft, Doug DelPrete, Charles Diamond, Paul Dubroff, Jim Edlin, Robert Fogler, George Fowler, Bob Frankston, Vincent Gale, Drew Gillett, Joel Goldstick, Paul Grant, Mal Greene, Roger Greenwall Jr., Joseph Guay, Richard Harris, Daniel Helman, Thomas Henry, Kenneth Heyne, David Hill, Phil Hopkins, Richard Hutchins, James Jackson, Harry Jacobson, Naomi Karten, Darryl Keith, Jeff Levering, F. B. Lothrop Jr., Miller Lovett, Ralph Luby, J. F. Maguire, Naomi Mallinson, Donald Martell, Hugh Mason, R. L. Massard, John McHugh, Lou McKinney, Edwin Meyer, Patrice Miller, George Nardi, Peter Nelson, James Ptrupczewski, John Roberts, Norman Ross, Brian Scarbeau, Art Schneiderman, Donna Senna, Nicholas Senzamici, Howard Shaffer, Joel Shaw, Robert Shorey, Dave Siktberg, Marjory Skinner, William Smith, Harry Snyder, Jack Staller, Steve Stansel, Thomas Stark, Cliff Sterns, Paul Stokinger, Jane Tamlyn, Avram Tetewsky, Mark Truelove, Edgar VanCott, and Joel Zimet.

Several people deserve special recognition for their help in putting together specific sections of the book. For his work on the sections on hard disks, data communications, and modems, thanks to Doug Chamberlin, head of the software exchange of our IBM PC user's group. The printer chapter was helped along by

Brian Camenker, a free-lance programmer and contributing editor of *PC Report,* our IBM newsletter; Glenn Fund, manager of the microcomputer resources center of GCA Corporation; and Bob Murray, Patrick Murray, and Eric Carroll of the Printer Port, a dealer in Dedham, Massachusetts. For his help with the data base chapter, thanks go to Joe Gannon, freelance data base consultant and sales representative for ComputerLand of Boston.

Assistance was frequently provided by members of the BCS staff: Jack Hodgson, Mary McCann, Rosemary O'Neil, and Anne Cochran. Coordinating assistance came from our board of directors, from Mike Rohrbach, coordinator of our IBM user group, and from Doug Chamberlin.

One additional group deserving special thanks are the five BCS members who read the first draft of the manuscript and offered valuable suggestions for its improvement: Art Bevilacqua, Bill Hartman, Fr. David Murphy, Louise Rijk, and Howard White.

We hope you enjoy this taste of the BCS and get a lot of useful information from it. If you're interested in getting more involved in the BCS, I can highly recommend the experience! To find out about joining the BCS, just give us a call at 617–367–8080 or write:

The Boston Computer Society
One Center Plaza
Boston, MA 02108

1 / It's Not You, It's IBM

They [corporations] cannot commit
treason, nor be outlawed, nor
excommunicated, for they
have no souls.

Sir Edward Coke, *Case of Sutton's Hospital*

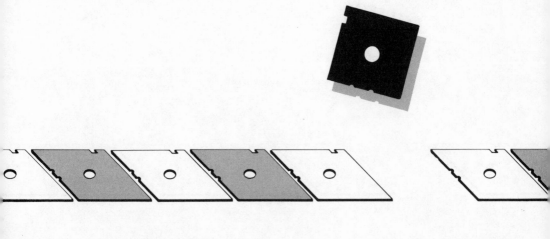

One January night in Wellesley, Massachusetts, during a discussion of this book, Bob Frankston, coinventor of VisiCalc, the program that kicked off the so-called microcomputer revolution, suggested we call the book "It's Not You, It's IBM."

His suggestion led to several minutes of enthusiastic commentary about IBM and some of the things it has done that pass comprehension. Why, for example, is there still a cassette port on the IBM PC? (And watch out that you don't plug the keyboard into the cassette port when you are setting up the machine. That's one of the few things you can do that really will damage your hardware.)

Basically, when they launched the PC, IBM's designers saw the machine as an imitation Apple II+. They didn't expect anyone to want a machine that had more than 64K. They did some things right—for example, they violated a few of the central tenets of the IBM canon and let outside firms develop software and they offered an expandable motherboard. They also did other things in ways that are unfathomable.

The important point to remember, particularly for a newcomer to the PC, is this: when something seems to have gone wrong, it is just as likely that you did exactly what you were told to do (or what seemed perfectly sensible to do) as it is that you failed to follow instructions.

We were searching for an example of that point when exactly the kind of "accident" happened that we are talking about. This book was written entirely on a PC. The word processing program used to write it uses the Ctrl key with the arrow keys to move forward or backwards one word at a time. As one of the authors composed the preceding paragraph, he reached for the Ctrl and the right arrow keys, but hit the Shift and PrtSc keys instead. The printer wasn't on line, but that doesn't matter to the machine; it looks for the printer, and if it is off line (that is, if it is not powered up, the cable is incorrectly attached, or the on-line switch on the printer has been turned off), rather than report the printer's status and return control to the keyboard, the machine continues to look— for between 45 seconds and a minute (or longer on some compatibles). While it is looking, everything comes to a halt: the program stops responding entirely, and you get the feeling that the system has crashed. The fault is in the keyboard's design and in the lack of a message alerting the user that the printer is off line. You can argue that the problem was with the user, but it's equally arguable that it was with IBM.

The experienced user comes to recognize the symptoms of such gaffes, though they can be disconcerting to the newcomer. The experienced user has learned to wait a while before taking such drastic action as turning off the power and restarting the machine.

Another annoyance voiced at that meeting concerned the lack of standards and compatibility. Nobody is setting standards, said one of the participants, especially not IBM. It's like the early days of the automobile industry; you just won't find many interchangeable parts. It would be helpful if everyone agreed, for example, on how a printer and a computer should communicate with each other and how modems should check the accuracy of data transmission. What does a lack of standards mean to you? In brief, it means that when that great new piece of hardware or software appears—the one that will make all the difference to you—there's a relatively good chance that you won't be able to use it or that using it will mean making major changes in how you use your machine or in the machine itself.

Who Needs This Book?

There will be times when you will question whether these machines are really worth the effort. You are not alone. Like any new technology or skill, using a computer can be confusing; it takes time and experience before the investment pays off.

When you have the good fortune to belong to a user group as large and as active as The Boston Computer Society (The BCS has close to 20,000 members and has 9,000 members in the IBM Special Interest Group; at least one and sometimes two user interest-group meetings or software or hardware clinics are in session every day but Sunday, almost every week of the year), you can always find someone to help you with a problem. When you are not that fortunate, you turn to books. Think of this book as your user group in absentia.

There is no substitute for the real thing, however. Join a local computer society. If you don't know where to locate one near you, go to a dealer and ask for the address of the nearest group. If the user group nearby is inactive, write:

IBM User Group Support
IBM Corporation 2900
P.O. Box 3022
Boca Raton, FL 33432

They'll tell you the number of their IBM user group phone line and bulletin board, so you can log into it directly.

Much of this book solves some ordinary problems, helps you get around some limitations of the more popular software—such as Lotus' 1-2-3 and WordStar—and shows you a few tricks that the manuals don't cover. A large number of the tips and tricks you'll find here have arisen from the direct experience of users.

Throughout the book you'll find comments or ideas in the margins ranging from general observations to detailed technical advice. These tips have been drawn almost entirely from the 150 or so responses to a questionnaire sent to a randomly selected group of 250 members of the IBM User Group of The Boston Computer Society.

Not everything in the book will be equally accessible to you. Some sections may be too elementary, some too advanced, depending on how you have invested your time in microcomputers. For example, you may have used only word processors and be only passingly familiar with spreadsheets. If so, you may find valuable things in the spreadsheet chapter. Six months from now, you may be ready for a part of the book that as far as you're concerned today might as well be written in Sanskrit.

One last comment before we launch: This is a book by users for users. If you are one of the sometimes perplexed but truly intrigued PC users, we hope that you will profit from our experiences.

Tip 1:

Record Keeping

Keep a log. I can go weeks without using the machine. At first, I found myself repeating my mistakes. A log helps minimize that.

The Laws of Problem Solving

The first law of problem solving on the PC is this: Read the manual first. It's similar to the first law of happy computing with the PC: Make a back-up copy immediately (if not sooner). Both are more honored in the breach than in fact.

Manuals were once truly execrable. They have improved immensely in the last few years, though there are still some problem areas. Reading documentation is an art, and like all arts it demands dedication and practice, practice, practice. In theory, no one writes technical documentation until the hardware or software specs are frozen. Documentation is—again in theory—the last step in the development process. In fact, long after the documentation is finished (or at least after its contents are frozen), people continue to fiddle with the code or the hardware specs. One technical writer has described the process of writing manuals as being similar to changing a flat tire on a moving car.

The second law of problem solving is this: When in doubt, read the manual. This law seems to apply more to experienced users than to novices. One BCS member tells of a night he, with the president of a local station of a major telecommunications network and another user, tried to connect to the user's new account on the network. They checked that the modem, a Hayes 1200 SmartModem, had all its switches set correctly, attached it to the phone and a Compaq, and got nowhere. After an hour of trying one thing and another, someone thought to look in the manual of the communications software they were using (CrossTalk) and discovered that the factory settings of the modem had to be changed to work with that software.

The third law is this: Persist. Few software and hardware developers, especially for the IBM, ship completely untested products. Before writing it off and returning it to the dealer, assume that somebody, somewhere, has managed to get it to do what it alleges. Don't assume that because something works once it will work twice. Conversely, if it didn't work the first time, give it a second try.

The fourth law is this: It's not as bad as it sounds. In other words, relax. The people who write error messages for computers lack perspective, which leads to such messages as "fatal error." (Our favorite error message, which you will not see when using a PC, was "fatal error on crawlout"; it gives you the impression that you almost got away with it—just another yard or two of open ground and you'd have triumphed.)

Tip 2:
Understanding the Manual

Don't think you're stupid if you can't read the manual.

Tip 3:
Reading the Manual

The corollary to the second law applies to new and old users alike: As you reread the manual, assume you did everything wrong.

Tip 4:

Error Terminology

"It's one thing to break a fingernail," says Bob Frankston, "but don't call it a 'fatal nail error.'" The tendency to issue such dire warnings is in keeping with a lot of the language that surrounds the PC. It is drawn from mayhem: you don't stop the system, you crash it or hang it; you don't retract a command, you abort it; you never scramble a disk's data, you trash it; you kill a file, bomb a program, fry a drive. Don't conclude from the language that you are perpetrating violence on those innocent chips every time you do something the machine doesn't like. That language is a sham. The machines are remarkably hardy and thick-skinned.

Hardware Help

Whenever you make a hardware change—for example, when you add a board or increase your computer's memory—run the diagnostics program that comes with your *Guide to Operations.*

When you run the diagnostics, you may see some error messages. They are somewhat cryptic, and the manual suggests that if you see any error message, you should repack the system unit and return it to the dealer. That's not always necessary, however.

For example, if you run the diagnostics while your printer is connected to the parallel port of a multifunction card rather than the parallel port on the display adapter, you will get message code 901. All that means is that your printer is not connected to the port that the diagnostic routines checked. Similarly, if you have nothing plugged into the asynchronous communications adapter port, you will get error code 1101.

Table 1-1 is a listing of the error codes and the parts of the system to which they refer. They aren't infallible; some error conditions may mask others and produce an error code that is inappropriate. The codes are relatively reliable, however, and they are a good starting point for troubleshooting.

Table 1-1: Error codes. An *x* represents a single-digit number.

Code	Possible Cause
02x	Power supply
1xx	System board
20xx or xzyy 20n	Memory
30x or xxx 30n	Keyboard
4xx	Monochrome display adapter
5xx	Color graphics display
6xx	Diskette drive
606	Disk drive or adapter failed
607	Diskette is write protected or write-protect electronics failed
611–623	Drive adapter or cable failure
621–626	Diskette drive failure
90x	Parallel printer adapter
110x	Asynchronous communications adapter
130x	Game controller adapter
140x	Printer
15xx	SDLC adapter
17xx	Hard disk drive
18xx	Expansion chassis
20xx	BSC adapter
parity check 1	Parity error in system board memory
parity check 2	Parity error in expansion board memory

If you decide to add memory chips to your system, be careful. Although adding chips is not a difficult task at all, you always run the risk of damaging one of the chips. Before you handle the chips, ground yourself by touching something metal. If you touch one of the pins on the

Tip 5:

Error Codes

Before you repack the system unit and lug it to a repair facility, call a dealer and ask if they can tell you the meaning of the error code you received. If the dealer has a copy of the IBM *Hardware Technical Reference* manual, you may save yourself a trip.

memory chip while you are carrying a static charge, you can burn out the chip. It won't give you any evidence that it has burned out, however. It won't smoke or smell, it just won't work and you'll have to replace it. Some users buy a few extra chips in case. When you insert the chip, take care that you don't bend the pins.

The error codes for bad memory are pretty clear. In the diagram of the system board (or mother board) shown in figure 1-1, the banks of RAM chips are outlined on the lower left. When

Figure 1-1: System Board
Component Diagram

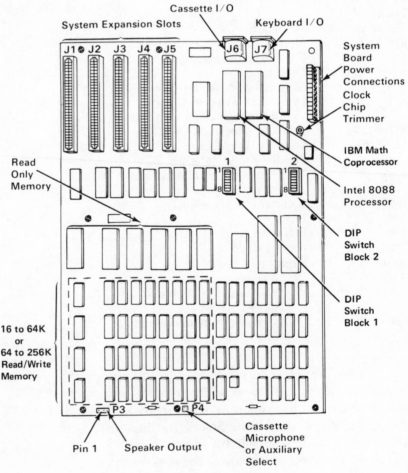

you run the system diagnostics, a bad chip will show up as a four-digit code. The first two digits identify the bank, and the last two identify the chip. Bank 0 is the farthest back of the four banks. Bank 3 is the closest.

The first two codes and the banks they represent are shown in table 1–2.

Table 1-2: First Two Digits of Error Codes for Bad Memory

Code		
PCI (64K)	PC2 (256K)	Bank
00	00	0
04	10	1
08	20	2
0C	30	3

The second two digits of the code tell you which chip is faulty. The codes begin with the parity chip—the first chip in the bank—and are numbered hexadecimally (that is, using base 16 rather than base 10). The first chip is 01, the second is 02, the third is 04, and so on (see table 1–3).

Table 1-3: Second Two Digits of Error Codes for Bad Memory

Chip	Code
parity	00
bit 0	01
bit 1	02
bit 2	04
bit 3	08
bit 4	10
bit 5	20
bit 6	40
bit 7	80

If the diagnostics give you code 3008, the suspect chip is in bank three, and is the fourth chip (not counting the parity chip). You can

Tip 6:

XT and IBM Portable Mother Boards

Some people don't notice that the XT and the IBM Portable have the same mother board. If you're adding an expansion board to the Portable, you can follow instructions that specify the XT.

Tip 7:

Testing

Test one thing at a time. Test it twice. If you tested it a week ago, don't assume it's still working correctly. In the span of a week, a drive can go from being aligned well enough to give a good test reading to being so seriously out of alignment that it will refuse to read a disk.

test that chip by removing it and one other chip (carefully) and swapping them. For example, if you get a 3008, try swapping that chip with the chip to its left; the error code should change to 2008. If you swap the bad chip with the chip in the same bank that is one chip closer to the parity chip, the code should read 3004.

Assumptions have a way of coming back to nip at your ankles. Double-check every step of the process when you add memory to your system. For example, the pins on a board can get bent under rather than seating properly in the socket. To play it extra safe, get a magnifying glass and make sure that all the pins are correctly seated. In addition, make sure that the notches on all the chips are lined up on the same side. Finally, always reset the system-board switches before you run the diagnostics. After all, if you don't tell the system what you've done, it will behave as though you haven't done anything.

When you run your PC, you are operating in a complex environment. Program A may run beautifully alone and with program B. It may also run beautifully with program C. One day you might run A, then B, and then C, and all will be well. On another day, you might run A, then C, then B, and odd little things will begin to happen. The programs may make subtly conflicting demands on the system—demands that the program developer could never have foreseen.

You can avoid wild goose chases if you remember never to make hardware and software changes at the same time. When you add a new board or a hard disk, don't also change your operating system and start using a new communications program. Remember, always test one thing at a time.

Tip 8:

Peripheral Compatibility

My most frustrating problem in the first six months was that my Tecmar Graphics Master board was not totally compatible with my Amdek 310A monitor, even though they work with the corresponding IBM equipment.

2/From Disks to Modems

How to save the old that's worth saving
. . . is one of our greatest problems, and
the one that we bother least about.

John Galsworthy, *Over the River*, Chap. 39

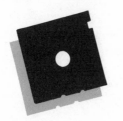

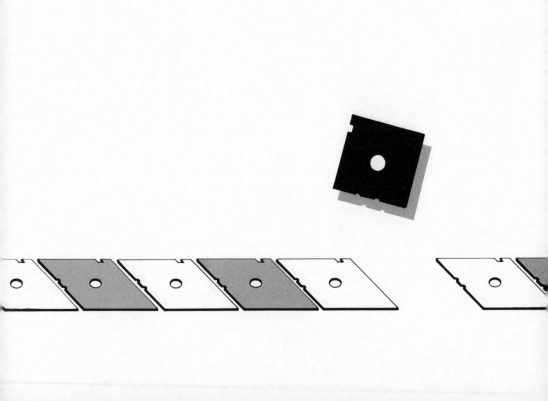

Before you turn off the power to your PC, you have to have some place to record the work you've been doing. That's mass storage; in the PC world, mass storage takes two forms—floppy disks and hard disks.

People whose computer experience predates the microcomputer remember punch cards and call the floppy disk the punch card of the 1980s. They also think floppies are a poor way to store data. Whether or not floppy disks are a good storage medium, for many PC users they are the only choice. Because the situation is likely to remain as it is for some time, you should spend a bit of time getting to know floppy disks better.

It's worth the two or three dollars that a disk costs to rip open a disk sleeve and see how the thing is constructed. There's usually a padding that separates the interior of the sleeve from the disk itself. The padding is heavily perforated, which maintains an air cushion between the disk itself and the sleeve while the disk is at rest. When the disk begins to rotate, the air cushion expands, minimizing the wear on the recording surface.

The disk sleeves of the diskettes used with an IBM PC and its compatibles contain several holes. The center hole, of course, is the hub hole, where the drive itself grasps the disk. A better-quality disk is usually reinforced at the hub. There is also a square cutout near the top of the disk—that is the write-protect notch. If it is not cut in the sleeve of the disk (which is the case with your DOS diskettes), you cannot write data or programs on the disk. Covering the write-protect notch with a tab also prevents anything from being written on the disk; a supply of tabs is often included in a box of diskettes.

It's usually a good idea to keep your write-

Tip 9:

Protecting Your Back-up Disk

If you have a problem, don't instantly take the disk out and put your only copy of something else in the drive. Stop and think through what you want to do—three times.

The Physical Side of Disks

protect tabs on all disks that contain programs, especially if the programs are copy protected. That prevents you from deleting or writing over files that are difficult or impossible to replace. To delete a file, the disk operating system must rewrite a portion of the "directory" of the diskette (see chapter 4); thus a write-protect tab also works as an erase-protect tab.

The small hole in the sleeve near the hub hole is the index hole. If you carefully turn the diskette within the sleeve, a smaller hole in the diskette itself will come into view. The hole in the disk is used as a reference point for the movement of the read and write heads in your disk drive. All the information that is recorded on the disk is given an address that is defined by its location relative to the index hole. When you ask for a file, if the index hole of the disk isn't already lined up with the index hole of the sleeve, the two are first aligned and then the information is read from the proper location. In soft-sectored disks (see "Tracks and Sectors," page 18), such as those used in the PC, there is one index hole in the disk. Hard-sectored disks contain index holes for each sector on the disk.

Finally, the oval hole at the bottom of the disk sleeve is the read-write hole. It is through this hole that the heads actually make contact with the disk and read or record magnetic impulses.

The Organizational Side of Disks

As you have learned by now, there are a single-sided and double-sided disk drives. Double-sided drives contain two read-write heads, one positioned above and the other beneath the disk. That's why there is a read-write hole on each side of the diskette. (To some degree, IBM's choice of single-sided drive in the first PCs sent to market is a bit of a mystery. The most reasonable, though speculative, explanation is that the company wanted to keep the price of the PC competitive with the Apple II+, which at that time dominated the market.) Only rarely do people still buy PCs with single-sided drives. In spite of that, suppliers continue to do a brisk business selling single-sided disks.

Actually, there are no differences between the manufacture of single-sided, single-density disks and that of double-sided, double-density disks. Any differences between them are established in the quality control process. In quality control, each disk is passed through a certifier, and a signal is recorded on every sector. The signal is then read back. If the certifier finds that the signal was properly recorded on every sector, the disk is designated as a double-sided, double-density disk. If a disk shows a flaw on one side, it is designated a single-sided, double-density disk. If it is flawed on both sides but is still usable, it becomes a single-sided, single-density disk.

Tip 10:

Single-sided Disks

When you format a disk for use on an IBM PC (or XT or AT) the formatting program locks out any bad sectors, thus preventing you from recording data on them. The remaining sectors, regardless of which side can be used, are recorded at any density. As a consequence, if you are so inclined, you can save a few dollars by buying single-sided, single-density disks for everyday use.

Don't use single-sided disks for back-up, though. When you are attempting to protect yourself against loss of data, using a disk you know to be flawed simply does not make sense. Use double-sided, double-density disks. They are more costly, but compared to the time you might require to recreate a lost file, the marginal extra cost is negligible.

One point should be made about back-ups and disks: if you have a fire in the office, you know that it has occurred and that you've probably lost some records. Magnetism, however, is an ephemeral medium, and you can have a small magnetic "fire" in the office without ever knowing it happened. Our physical environment is saturated with electromagnetic impulses that are completely invisible but that are present no matter where you have stored your back-up disks (for example, a compass points to magnetic north whether you are indoors or out). Over time, even if virtually nothing seems to have happened, environmental magnetic phenomena can cause magnetically stored data to deteriorate. Thus, if you have archived data or programs and haven't used them for a year to 18 months, it's probably prudent to transfer the files to newly formatted (if not actually new) diskettes and to reformat the old disks.

Tracks and Sectors

On each side of the diskette is a region on which data can be recorded. When you format a diskette, that region is organized into tracks: discrete, concentric rings, each of which is a specific distance from the hub. A disk typically contains 40 tracks (though there can be as many as 80), which are numbered from 0 to 39.

Finding data on a diskette is one of the slowest operations your PC performs. Each time you change data you must record its new value, and that means that your disk drive must find the track where the data has been stored. This operation would be even slower if the entire track had to be re-recorded each time a change was made. What's more important, though, is that you would only be able to place one file on each track. Consequently, tracks are further subdivided into sectors, each of which may contain from 128 to 1,024 bytes of data.

Whenever you save a file, regardless of its

size, it is stored in whole sectors. In the IBM, each sector generally stores 512 bytes, but each sector also uses some storage space to manage the sector itself. Whether the file is 2 or 512 bytes long, it uses an entire sector. If it is 514 bytes long, it uses two sectors. When you use the DIRectory command, you are told how many bytes of storage remain on the diskette. If, however, you delete a file that is, say, 3,478 bytes long, you may regain more than 3,478 bytes of storage space.

At one time, hard-sectored disks were more widely used than soft-sectored ones. A hard-sectored disk is one in which each sector is identified by an index hole near the hub. The problem was that soft-sectored disks required a more expensive disk-controller card than did hard sectored disks. Thus, the cost of circuitry determined the kind of disk used. As usual in the microcomputer field, circuitry costs dropped and now there's no price advantage to hard sectoring. At one time, it was also generally the case that hard-sectored disks offered more storage space than soft-sectored disks. Now, data-organization schemes and hardware have made it possible to store as much as 1,200,000 bytes (1.2 megabytes) of data on a soft-sectored disk.

When you store a file, the disk operating system finds the first available sector and begins recording the file there. If the file needs more than one sector and the adjacent sector is available, the next 512 bytes of the file are stored there. If the sector adjacent to the first is occupied by a file, the operating system stores the next 512 bytes in the next available sector. When a diskette is new, each file is stored in a series of contiguous sectors. After a while, however, if you have changed, erased, and resaved several of the files on the disk, they will have begun to fragment. You will have no trouble recalling any of them, but the time it takes to do so will increase. If you are using a program that

Tip 11:

DISKCOPY Advice

DISKCOPY copies the disk sector by sector, making an exact replica of a disk. If the disk is fragmented, DISKCOPY will make a new, fragmented disk. For the most part, the only time you should use DISKCOPY is when you must have an exact replica of the disk to examine sectors that you may have erased and want to restore.

reads the disk frequently, as some data base and word-processing programs do, you'll find that it takes more time to read files, because the heads must seek out widely separated parts of the disk. To restore the files to contiguous sectors, simply copy them to a fresh disk. Don't use "DISKCOPY", however. Instead, use "COPY *.*", which will copy all the sectors of a given file before copying the next file. Making a file-by-file copy of the disk eliminates fragmentation (if the disk to which you are writing the copies is new).

Never make a hardware and a software change at the same time. Should something go wrong—and something always does—you will have too many variables to test to find the problem.

Similarly, when you begin using a computer, and until you are very familiar with it, don't economize on disks. A low-quality disk can cause problems that look like software problems. After you are accustomed to your machine and to your software, you can switch to low-cost, potentially troublesome disks if you desire.

Tip 12:

Saving Work and DOS Shells

Try to avoid being in the middle of a program and finding out that you have no formatted disks to save your work on. Some programs—Symphony, for example—allow you to suspend the program, give commands to the operating system, and resume working on the file you'd left. That ability to "open a DOS shell" allows you to format a disk, check the directory of a disk, or even run another program. Not many programs allow you to do that, however. Alternatively, utility programs such as Sidekick or Spotlight allow you to suspend a program you are running and issue commands to the operating system.

Back-ups

The general rule of backing up—that is, making additional copies of your files—is to do it early and do it often. Though occasionally a buggy program or a faulty piece of hardware reaches the market, the machines and programs are relatively "bulletproof." It is usually safe to do almost anything you wish on a microcomputer, especially if you do back-ups on a regular basis.

Many programs generate back-up files automatically or give you the option to make them automatically. Don't let that lull you into thinking that you have truly backed up a file. Most of such back-ups are on the same disks as the original, and that's not a good place to keep a back-up. Back-ups should be kept on different disks altogether.

Tip 13:

Storing Back-up Disks

Back-up disks should be kept in a different location. If they are office files, you should take the back-up copies home or to a different building, if your business is a multi-site operation. If they are your personal records, think about putting them in a safety deposit box at a bank if you don't want to take them to work. It may seem like a lot of trouble, but when something goes wrong the trouble you've taken is more than repaid.

Tip 14:

Backing Up for Problem Solving

When you get an error message involving reading or writing a disk, one of the first things you should do is make a back-up copy of whatever you are working on.

The BACKUP program that comes with DOS 2.x and 3.x is primarily for backing up a hard disk to diskettes. Many of the people who have used it regularly for a long time swear at it. In general their feeling is that a tape back-up is a better alternative (see "Backing Up the Hard Disk," later in this chapter).

Hard Disks

Changing Times

I wish I had a hard disk; handling diskettes gets to be a chore. It will still be necessary for back-ups when I do get the hard disk, though. We never had to face things like this before. MIS worried about it!

Most of us start out with machines that have one or more floppy disk drives. Although they serve admirably for a while, sooner or later many people feel cramped by the storage limits of floppies and begin to think about enlarging their machines' storage capacities.

Hard disks are one of the common solutions to the storage crunch. They provide larger storage capacity and faster access to data than do floppy disks. Before you buy a hard disk, however, make sure that you know exactly why you are buying it and what alternatives you have foregone.

There are a number of reasons to add storage capacity. Some of us simply tire of managing a growing collection of floppy diskettes. They can be difficult to catalog or index, but be aware that low-cost programs are available that will maintain a library-like catalog of all the files on all your disks. In short, don't invest in a hard disk if all you need is help keeping track of where you stored last month's memo to George—get yourself organized instead.

Some people look at the growing costs of all the floppy disks they accumulate and elect to put the money into a hard disk. First they should check that they are buying the appropriate quality of disks as cheaply as possible. Prices have been reduced significantly in the last year and continue to go down as manufacturing volumes go up. In addition, remember that you can use single-sided disks in many cases.

On occasion, one or more of your data files may grow beyond the capacity of its disk. That can be a real problem if you never planned to use anything but disks and your data volume just grew too fast. Although most programs do not allow for it, your software may allow you to split your file into separate pieces and store the different pieces on different disks. Even if that works, however, it is possible that all of the disks with the data will have to be on-line at the same time, and you may have too few disk drives to do that. In this instance, a hard disk may be imperative.

Be realistic about how much a hard disk will help you. A ten-megabyte hard disk (one of the most common sizes available) stores the approximate equivalent of forty floppy disks. Considering your growing disk library, that isn't too many. Most people find that ten megabytes isn't enough to store all the data they want to store; at the same time, ten megabytes of data is too much to use disks for the main back-up medium (more on hard-disk back-up in a moment).

Of course, ten megabytes isn't the only size for a hard disk. Some models will store up to three hundred megabytes, but cost and storage capacity are positively correlated. Generally, hard disks that store between twenty and forty megabytes yield the best cost-per-byte ratio. But shop around, because memory costs have historically been the most volatile in all kinds of computers, generally tending to head down at dizzying rates. Estimate your future needs carefully, remembering that you once thought that you could get by using only floppy disks.

If your programs are taking too long to process data, you may be able to speed things up by using a hard disk. Hard disks are generally two to twenty times faster than floppy disks, depending on the make and model. As a rule of thumb, the least expensive hard disks are the slowest because the faster access circuits cost a little more to design and build. The ten-megabyte disk drives used in the IBM PC XT are among the slower models.

Don't be too optimistic about how a speed

increase will solve your problems. Just as you outgrew floppy disk speeds, you may well outgrow hard disk speeds. In addition, don't judge the performance of a hard disk based on how it runs for the first few days. As you add files and programs to the disk, it will slow down noticeably. It will still outperform floppy disks, but the bloom will fade, and you may eventually wish that you could find a hard disk that is a bit faster.

One alternative to hard disks is higher-capacity disks. Some disk drives enable you to store 800K on a single disk, and the PC/AT can be equipped with 1.2-megabyte drives. Although that may be only twice the capacity you are used to, it may suit your needs. These disk drives often can read your current disks, so you automatically start with a back-up set of disks. However, they generally cannot write to disks that have been used with lower-capacity drives.

The prices of high-capacity disk drives are competitive so check them out. Be aware, however, that they are not officially supported by IBM on any of IBM's models except the IBM PC/AT, so some of your software may not run on these drives.

For only a little more than $100, you can install a new floppy disk drive that is identical to the original equipment. Hard disks cost more to replace and more to repair, so be prepared for higher repair bills in the event of a failure. You may want to consider a blanket service contract that covers you if anything goes wrong for a specified period of time. Such contracts are available from many nationwide service companies.

In summary, hard disk drives have distinct advantages over floppy disks in capacity and speed. It is important, however, to know that you are, in effect, putting all of your eggs in one basket and that you must therefore plan for adequate back-up and servicing procedures.

Hard Disks and Your Power Supply

Adding a hard disk to your system has ramifications for the power supply. In general, the larger the hard disk's capacity, the more power it will consume. In the absence of other peripherals, the PC usually has sufficient power to support a hard disk. Few users, however, have completely unpopulated mother boards (that is, few users have no boards installed in the system board), so the capacity of your power supply is a consideration.

At 5 volts the mother board uses 1.6 amps, the display card that runs your monitor takes about 1.3 amps, the floppy drive and its controller use 0.9, and a multifunction expansion board takes another 0.7. That adds up to 5.6 amps and leaves 1.4 for the hard disk controller and a ten-megabyte hard disk, which use approximately 1.7 and 1.5 amps respectively. That means that you've overloaded the power supply by about 1.2 amps. The machine may run well enough for a while, because the figures that IBM puts out concerning the power supply measure average demand, not peak load.

The figures above assume that you are using an internally mounted hard disk, thus using one of the bays that would otherwise be occupied by a floppy disk drive. If you are adding an external drive and will have two floppy drives and a hard disk, you will push your power requirements to slightly more than 9 amps.

External power supplies are available, and you should think about using one if you add a hard disk. That will jack up the cost initially, but if you don't pay now you could pay more later when the power supply dies and takes your data with it.

Backing Up the Hard Disk

Disks are convenient and easy-to-duplicate media. They protect your data well if you store

Tip 16:

Backing Up Hard Disks

Be sure you budget time to make back-up copies of your hard disk data files. It always takes longer than you think it will—and much longer than you'd like.

back-up copies in a safe place. Moreover, with a floppy disk system it is as easy to use the back-up as it is to use the original. Once you have converted to a hard disk, however, you will always need to use the hard disk—you won't have a spare. Consequently, you need to pay more attention to adequate back-up procedures than when you used floppy disks.

Some hard disks come with tape cartridge back-up systems. There are two fundamental types of tape back-up—streaming and non-streaming tape. Nonstreaming systems take longer to copy a given amount of data, because the tape must be started and stopped for every piece of data that is stored. That means that for most of the time in the back-up process, the tape is either stopped or accelerating to the correct speed for reading and/or writing data. An advantage of nonstreaming tape back-ups is that individual files can be written to the tape, and the software generally stores descriptive information about each file, enabling you to obtain a directory of the tape.

Streaming tapes, on the other hand, start once and then maintain the proper speed for a longer duration. Thus, data can be transferred to and from the tape faster. Streaming tapes have one major drawback, however. They must generally be used to back up an entire hard disk at one pass; you cannot usually elect to back up individual files. Correspondingly, you must also restore (the opposite procedure to backing up) the entire hard disk at one pass; you cannot get back just that one memo you backed up last week. Furthermore, a tape directory may not be available. Therefore, for selective file back-up it is sometimes desirable to use floppy disks in conjunction with streaming tapes.

Back-up copies of hard disk systems, like their counterparts for floppy systems, should be kept in a different location from the original.

Tip 17:

Ventilation

My Davong hard disk started dropping characters after a couple of hours of use. It turned out to be an overheating problem. I solved the problem by improving its ventilation.

Organizing a Hard Disk

The storage limit of a floppy disk is a virtue of a sort. Although you can put a respectable number of files on one floppy, it is still a relatively manageable number. A hard disk enables you to store more than thirty times as many files as can be kept on a floppy disk and thus presents you with the problem of organizing the disk.

There are no hard and fast rules for organizing the disk. Some people create subdirectories based on the programs they commonly use and then keep the programs and the appropriate data files in that directory. This method has the advantage of not using up space with multiple copies of the same program file.

Other people keep programs in one directory and organize the rest of the disk by project, product, month, or whatever natural division their activities dictate. If the programs you use don't support file names that include subdirectory delimiters, this may not be an option for you.

Whatever you choose, try to think not only about what you need today but about how you might change things in the future. The hard trick is changing file names. It can be a tedious process if you've got to do it for four or five hundred files. Remember that you are reconstructing your filing system. If what you are doing now works, then you may simply move it to the computer.

Between the floppy disk and the hard disk stands a device called the Bernoulli Box. A Bernoulli Box uses an eight-inch floppy disk encased in a ¾-inch cartridge. The floppy disk is read through a slot, but the read-write heads never come in contact with the disk. Unlike a smaller floppy disk, the disk in a Bernoulli Box can store ten megabytes of data; in addition,

Tip 18:

The Original PC and Hard Disks

If you are thinking of adding a hard disk to your 1982 PC, version 1, you need a ROM update kit.

Bernoulli Boxes

the Bernoulli Box can read and write data approximately twice as fast as the hard disk in an IBM XT. The Bernoulli Box contains two drives, one of which is used to back up the other, a process that takes 2½ minutes to accomplish, compared to an hour or so of backing up to floppy disks. A cartridge costs around $80, but it will hold approximately as much data as thirty floppies, which means that to store data on a cartridge costs roughly as much as to store it on floppies.

One disadvantage of the standard Bernoulli Box is that it cannot be partitioned the way that the hard disk on a PC can. A version of the Bernoulli Box, called the Bernoulli Plus, emulates the XT and allows partitioning. However, it also emulates the speed of the XT.

As of summer 1985, the only manufacturer of Bernoulli Boxes is Iomega Systems, in Utah.

Data Communications

Many industry observers feel that data communications will provide the vehicle for the most valuable applications for personal computers. That is because data communications opens the world to you just as the telephone did for voice communications.

You need four things to get started in data communications: a modem, a way to hook it to your computer, software that operates with it, and another computer to talk to.

A modem turns data characters into a variable tone that can be transmitted over telephone lines. The process is analogous to a printer turning ASCII characters into printed letters. When a second modem is connected to the first modem, the second one listens to the variations in the tone and interprets them, translating the tone back into characters. Of course, a modem can both send and receive signals.

Both the sending and the receiving modem must be designed to generate or listen for tones of a certain frequency. Some modems can select between different frequencies and can, therefore, communicate with a variety of other modems. The terms used to describe the two most common frequencies are *300 baud* and *1200 baud.* At 300 baud, a modem is transmitting approximately 30 characters per second. A 1200-baud modem, as the name implies, sends data at four times the rate of a 300-baud modem.

Most modems used today—and all of those selling for under $100—are 300-baud modems. A 1200-baud modem is always more expensive than a 300-baud modem. Until recently, they were much more expensive, but as they grew more popular, their prices fell; now they are roughly twice as expensive as 300-baud models.

Modems can be connected to your computer in two common ways. Some modems connect via cable to the serial, or RS–232, port that is already part of your machine. Those modems are external and are usually in a housing that allows you to place them directly beneath a standard telephone. Some modems are not enclosed in a housing, but come as a circuit board that is mounted internally in a vacant slot on the mother board.

Data communications software is widely available. Most of the programs share the same basic features and, like word-processing software, each program has its die-hard lovers and haters. There are, however, a few features that might be considered essential to a good data communications program. The most important feature is file-at-a-time transfer. Because *connect-time*—the time you spend actually using a communications line—costs at least $5 or $6 an hour, and sometimes as much as $150 an hour, it's most economical to compose and edit docu-

Tip 19:

Communications Costs Tradeoffs

Using the telephone lines costs money, as does using the carrier's computer at the other end of the line. Transmitting data at 300 baud takes roughly four times as long as transmitting the same data at 1200 baud, so your savings on equipment may be completely offset by higher connect-time charges.

If you are thinking of data communications that will entail the transmission of numerous long documents, it may well pay to choose the higher speed modem. On the other hand, it is a bargain only if you really need the higher performance in the first place.

ments when you are not connected. File-at-a-time transfer permits you to transmit a file you composed off-line.

Another important feature is a conversation mode, one in which anything you type at the keyboard is immediately transmitted through the modem and anything the modem receives is immediately displayed on your screen.

A third important feature is the combination of error-detection and XMODEM file-transfer protocol. Error-detection is used during file-transfer to detect if a transmission failure has occurred. The XMODEM protocol is a particular method of error-detection that allows the receiving computer to request that the transmitting computer repeat any parts of the transmission that did not get through correctly. Although XMODEM is only one of many protocols that perform that function, it is a widely used and popular standard.

Another valuable feature is *data capture,* which allows you to copy to a disk or printer all transmitted and received data; you can then review it later.

The biggest thing to consider here is what your primary uses will be. You don't want your shiny new modem to sit unused because of lack of available remote systems. You also do not want it to go unused because the remote system you intended to communicate with has incompatible equipment. As was pointed out above, 300-baud modems cannot talk to modems that are set to receive at 1200 baud. Furthermore, software that uses XMODEM protocol for file-transfer cannot send files to software that uses another protocol. Check out the potential remote systems you may use and be sure to get equipment that is compatible.

One final note: many personal computers owners use their systems to provide the public with "bulletin board" services. That is, they leave their computers turned on, waiting for the phone to ring. When it does ring, the computer answers the phone and talks to any other computer that has called. The software that is running on these "bulletin board" machines enables the caller to leave messages addressed to one or more other callers, who later dial up to read their messages. In addition, files can be transmitted to the bulletin board system (uploaded) and later retransmitted (downloaded) to another caller.

These bulletin board systems are one of the big reasons personal computer owners get into data communications. They are fun to use and a valuable information exchange between people with similar interests.

3/Printers

Then the black-bright, smooth-running, clicking clean
Brushed, oiled and dainty typewriting machine,
With tins of ribbons waiting for the blows
Which soon will hammer them to verse and prose.

John Masefield, *Shopping in Oxford*

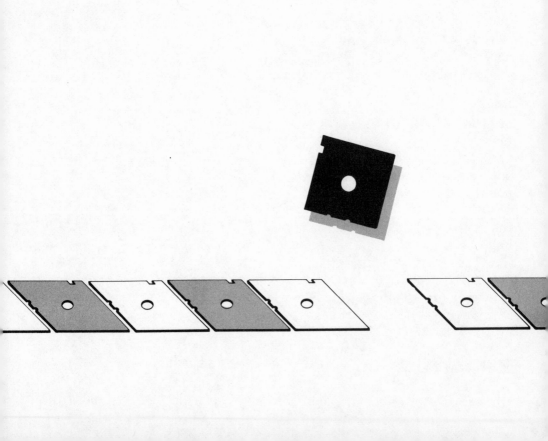

A disk drive is a disk drive, and it doesn't make much difference whether you run Lotus' 1-2-3 or Rbase 4000 in a Tandon, a CDC, or a Teac drive. The programs run and do all the things they were designed to do. Printers, however, are different. A printer may not be capable of doing all the things a piece of software can demand of it. The opposite is also true: a printer may have far more capacity than a piece of software can exploit.

Printers can be grouped into two general classes: impact and nonimpact printers. Impact printers, as their name suggests, produce images on paper by means of some mechanism that actually strikes the paper. The three most common mechanisms used by impact printers are dot matrix, daisy wheel, and thimble.

On a letter-quality printer, a hammer fires out of the head and strikes a petal on either a daisy wheel or a thimble. The petal contains a fully formed individual character.

In contrast, the print head of a dot matrix printer contains a set of pins—usually seven, eight, or nine—arranged in a stack. As the print head travels across the paper, the pins are fired at the ribbon, leaving the image of a letter behind.

Nonimpact printers produce images without striking the paper. The three most common nonimpact printing devices employ ink jets, lasers, or thermal print heads. Figure 3–1 shows the mechanisms used by both impact and nonimpact printers.

A laser printer creates the image on paper by exposing the surface of an electrostatically sensitive drum to a pattern of high-energy light and applying a toner that adheres to the drum's exposed surfaces and is then transferred to a

Impact and Nonimpact Printers

Tip 20:

Printers and Word-processing Software

Printers can be especially sensitive to the kind of word processing software that you use. For that reason your decision about a printer and word processing software should usually be made as one decision, though rarely does life work like that.

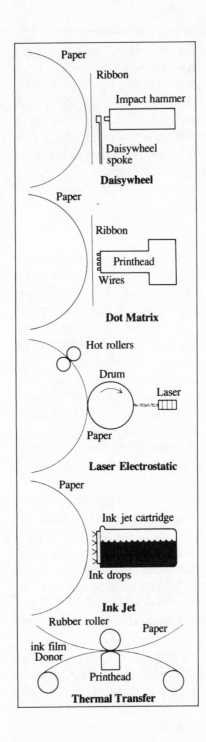

Figure 3-1: Mechanisms used by impact and nonimpact printers

sheet of paper. It is similar to xerography, except that it produces an original image, not a copy.

Thermal printers produce images by applying heat to specially treated paper that darkens where it is heated or by heating a ribbon that transfers the image to paper. The thermal print head is similar to a dot matrix print head, but instead of firing, the pins conduct heat to the paper. Unheated pins cause no image.

An ink jet printer produces images by spraying an electronically controlled stream of ink onto paper from a print head that travels across the paper.

Impact printers represent older technologies. The dot matrix printer, for example, has been around for a decade. Daisy wheel and thimble printers are newer, but are essentially adaptations of typewriter print elements. Nonimpact printers are of more recent technological vintage. Which should you choose?

The advantage of a nonimpact printer is that it's silent. In an office environment, that can be important. If you can find a nonimpact printer that's reasonably fast and gives reasonable print quality, it should serve you well. Right now (mid 1985), unfortunately, ink jet, thermal, and laser printers aren't quite ready for wide use.

Thermal printers have never taken off, perhaps because of the paper they use. It is silvery gray and has a very hard surface. It is also expensive, compared to other papers. Thermal transfer printers use normal paper. The image is transferred to the paper by the selective heating of portions of the print head as it passes over a ribbon. They, too, seem to have had a limited appeal, possibly because of the reputation that thermal printers in general gained earlier.

Laser printers are expensive, though their prices are heading down. Besides the disadvantage of being costly, laser printers won't do multipart forms, although they run so fast that you can generate five or eight copies of a form as quickly as you can print one page on an impact printer. The laser printer would also eliminate the "press hard, you're making four copies" sort of form. This might not always be good. For example, there are times when you want a carbon copy of the signature; people might not appreciate having to sign their names four times.

Ink jet printers are worth watching. Their biggest drawback is that they cannot use regular, everyday bond paper: unless special paper is used, the print quality is poor. If you use off-the-shelf bond paper, the ink bleeds or tends to splash, and a kind of grayish area appears around the copy. Every ink jet printer available now needs a special paper. With that paper they do well, although they are sometimes sensitive to stray static electricity in the air or ionizing devices, such as air cleaners. If you want to use preprinted forms, you'll pay exorbitant prices to have them printed on the special paper. Ink jet printers are also unable to do multipart forms, because there's no impact to produce the second and third impressions. If ink jet technology is improved to the point that ink can be fired on ordinary paper, producing good-looking output, then the dot matrix printer market will suffer.

For the immediate future, daisy wheel and thimble printers will be the first casualties of improved printer technology. For one thing, they cannot print graphics, so if you need to print a pie chart or a scatter diagram, you cannot possibly consider daisy wheels or thimbles. The real threat to the daisy wheel or thimble printer, however, will come initially, not from laser, ink jet, or thermal printers, but from dot matrix printers.

Dot matrix printers have improved so much that you can now use them for most applications, including correspondence. It used to be that a clear line could be drawn between letter-quality and draft-quality printing, but now it's possible to define three classes of printing: draft, correspondence, and presentation quality.

Figure 3–2 shows a page printed with one of the newer dot matrix printers, the Toshiba 1351, including an enlarged view of the characters produced by the Toshiba and those produced by an IBM Selectric typewriter using a film and a cloth ribbon.

The difference between the Toshiba 1351 and other dot matrix printers on the market is that is uses 24 pins—two banks of 12 pins each—and moves the print head a very short distance between firings. As a consequence, the pin patterns are very tight. You pay for that technology, however; the Toshiba, at a list price of nearly $1,800, is among the most expensive of the dot matrix printers.

In general, dot matrix printer manufacturers have listened to all the things that the market has been telling them. The machines are becoming quieter, faster, and better, and the prices are coming down.

Wide- versus Narrow-carriage Printers

Do you really need a wide-carriage printer? Sometimes people deliberately buy more printer capacity than they currently need, looking two or three years ahead. However, even if you print a lot of wide spreadsheet models, you may not need a wide printer. For one thing, you can print the spreadsheet in compressed type (17 characters per inch as opposed to 10 or 12, the standard widths of pica and elite type). That enables you to print columns *A* through *M* (at 9 characters per column) on an 8½-inch-wide sheet. You can also buy software, such as Sideways, that enables you to print spreadsheet

TOSHIBA P1351

Dear Customer,

Purchasing a printer for your computer system can be a major investment. With careful selection of the printer that fits your needs you will be able maintain an extremely productive office system.

First, of all you want to choose a printer with a strong reliability record, a printer that will not fail when you need it most.   Secondly you want to examine which printing features complement your needs. Do you need fast throughput? How about letter quality printing? Maybe variable print fonts? Do you have a need for graphics?

Upon careful consideration of your needs the chances are you will find that all of these features are required to develop a complete office computing system. The Toshiba P1351 dot-matrix printer fulfills all of these needs.   It provides reliability, speed, quality, and graphics all in one unit.   That lends itself well to another business consideration: price.   The Toshiba P1340 offers all of these qualities at an economical price.

PRINTING FEATURES

* 192 Character per second draft printing
* 93 Character per second letter quality print
* Prestige Elite Letter Quality Font
* Courier Letter Quality Font
* ^{super}scripts and $_{sub}$scripts
* <u>Continuous</u> <u>underlining</u>
* Microspace justification capability

Once installed, the P1351 will be one component you will not soon outgrow. In addition to the standard features you can expand your P1351 with some of its useful options. If you have a need for continuous forms, you can use the optional bidirectional pin feed tractor or for even greater paper handling you can use the optional automatic sheet feeder. If you decide you need additional letter quality fonts, just incorporate the available disk fonts and download them to your printer for even more versatility.

It is only logical that a high quality printer such as this Toshiba P1351 would be one of the products available from PRINTER PORT. We offer a large variety of output devices to fit a wide variety of small business needs.   In addition we offer complete service to back all of our sales, from hardware to software, from technical support to advice. Our showroom is located in the rear of the East Dedham Shopping Plaza and we suggest that you call for directions.   Our business hours are 10:00-6:00 Monday thru Wednesday and Friday; 10:00-9:00 on Thursday and 10:00-4:00 on Saturday.   We hope that we can be of service to you.

Figure 3-2: Output of the Toshiba 1351

models along the long axis of the paper. With such software, the limiting factor is the depth of the model you want to print—that is, whether it extends beyond row 50 or so of the spreadsheet. If so, you'll have to cut and paste whatever you do.

The maximum number of characters you can fit on a horizontally printed line is 235 (that's 17 characters per inch on 13 $7/8$-inch paper, the standard width for a wide carriage printer). The practical maximum number of lines you can print is 88 to 110, or 8 to 10 lines per vertically printed inch. Any more and you will begin printing lines over each other. Those maximums, of course, assume that you are printing from edge to edge and top to bottom of the page. If you add margins, the maximums will be reduced.

If you rarely use a spreadsheet or if your spreadsheet models can be condensed and made to fit on a page without looking cramped or hard to read, then you probably do not need a wide-carriage printer.

The real problems with printers arise from the ways that different programs use them. The printer must receive its signals in a particular way; if a program sends the printer signals in odd or unexpected ways, you have a printer problem that cannot be solved by fiddling with the printer, although that is where many people look to find the solution. One of the easiest ways around many such printer problems is to stick with the printers that are most popular, an Epson or Okidata dot matrix or a NEC Spinwriter letter-quality printer. Those are the ones that software developers keep in mind when they write the printer-control code sections of their programs and that they are least willing to ignore when they release a version of their pro-

Software Sensitivity

Tip 21:

Printer Frustration

The most frustrating thing in the first six months was printer interfacing—and remembering to back up files.

grams. On the other hand, the popularity of those printers has enforced a sort of standard on other manufacturers, who must make their machines behave like the ones the marketplace has made into leaders.

Experienced printer specialists say that it's not unusual to find people who have defined their needs well in certain areas but who have overlooked the impact of the software they've bought. For example, they may know that they want a letter-quality printer that runs a minimum of 15 characters per second; that they have x letters a day to get out; that they want to be able to include a particular set of print characteristics in the letters; and that the printer should be within a certain price range. All well and good, but if they have already bought a word-processing program, they may suddenly find they have no printer choice whatever, because only one printer will do what they want with that program.

Matching the printer and the software is a matter of dealing with different drivers. A driver is a program that controls an input or output device. Your keyboard is an input device, and although you do not see it, part of the operating system you use is a program called the keyboard driver. There are printer drivers, disk-drive drivers, keyboard drivers, and so on. Most of the more popular word-processing packages aren't a problem, because they come with a selection of drivers for different printers. Those drivers might be invisible to you if the word-processing program has an accompanying installation program. Such an installation program will ask what kind of printer you have connected to the system and will then use the correct driver for that printer, if available.

Under ideal circumstances, you should find your word processing software even before you buy a microcomputer. Because there is a wide

Tip 22:

Printer Drivers

If your word processor does not list your printer as an option, you may be in for a bout of frustration. If the program does not require you to run an installation routine, check for files on the disk that have names that resemble printer names (for example, OKI, EPS, or NEC for Okidata, Epson, and NEC printers) or that end in a suffix similar to prt. Those files are the printer drivers, and you will have to make one of them active, probably by changing its name somehow. The method for doing that should be in the manual.

selection of word processors for the IBM PC, however, you aren't likely to be penalized by first purchasing the machine. The second step is to decide on the image you want to present and the speed with which you want to present it. That will tell you which printer to buy.

A really good typist can type 100 words per minute. The average word is five characters, so a really good typist puts 500 characters on a sheet of paper every minute. That translates into more than eight characters per second. Very slow printers run at 13 to 15 characters per second (cps). We all know that printers are faster than the best typists, but what does that mean? In a practical sense, it means that you are likely to use much more paper and many more ribbons than you did when you traveled the low-tech road of typing documents. The capability to produce a copy of a document quickly tends to encourage users to produce them often. Printers take as much paper and as many ribbons as typewriters used to. We marvel at how much more productive the microcomputer has made us, but we often overlook how much more we pay for that productivity in terms of supplies consumed.

The expense of supplies sometimes leads to a lot of corner cutting and some false economies. One is the strategy of reinking your ribbon. Reinking a ribbon seems to be a reasonable way to save a few dollars, especially now that you are producing four to six printed pages for every two you produced when they had to be typed. What is sometimes overlooked, though, is that most printer ribbon inks contain a lubricant as well as pigments. On a dot matrix printer, the ribbon remains in constant contact with the print head. If the lubricant is gone from the rib-

Supplies: The Hidden Cost

Tip 23:

Freezing the Ribbon

The trick of putting a ribbon cartridge in the freezer overnight to redistribute the ink doesn't work with Epson cartridges. It's probably ineffective for all ribbons.

Tip 24:

Printer Supplies

The printer industry is similar to the razor business: the original items are cheap, but the supplies keep you going back to the shop.

bon, it becomes effectively a piece of emery cloth, wearing the pins down on the head. If you use the proper ink, fine. If not, you'll end up spending money on a print head sooner than you might have otherwise. (On a letter quality printer, of course, there's less of a wear factor.)

Printer-ribbon prices have risen as printer prices decreased. It used to be that printers cost $12,000 or $15,000, and as a proportion of costs, ribbons were negligible. As printer technology advanced, printers required better-quality ribbons made of sturdier material and longer-lasting inks. Prices naturally went up. In the business environment today, if you use a printer eight hours a day, ribbon costs may make up 20 to 25 percent of the cost of the hardware per year. Thermal printer ribbons are costly, though the printers themselves are cheap, so thermal ribbons could cost almost as much each year as the printer itself cost initially.

In response to this problem, Panasonic has begun using a cartridge that exposes only a small portion of the ribbon. The cartridge can even be re-inked by the push of a button. The usual life of a ribbon is 1,000,000 characters; Panasonic is claiming that its cartridge will last for 3,000,000 characters.

If you buy a letter-quality printer, you will eventually have to replace your daisy wheel or thimble. Plastic daisy wheels are much less expensive than metal ones, but they break sooner. When they do break, though, you know it at once. Metal daisy wheels and thimbles start out by bending, and the letters get out of line. Sometimes that's not noticeable right away, but you can check for a roller-coaster effect by placing a ruler along the top of the printed line. If some letters reach the ruler and some don't, the thimble, the wheel, or possibly even the print head is showing wear. The question then is whether you should replace it with a metal or plastic one. The best advice on that score is not to buy metal unless you know it will last three to four times as long as plastic, and only experience can tell you that. User-group members will often have tried enough different options to provide the help you need.

Buying and Servicing

More things can go wrong with a printer than with any other part of the system, except possibly disk drives. Because they have moving parts that are subject to wear and tear, they tend to break down more often than purely electronic devices. That's one of the reasons for buying a printer from a dealer rather than through the mail; you have someone to bring it back to and to listen to your complaints. (That has psychological value, too.)

Buy such supplies as ribbons as cheaply as you can, but not too cheaply. If a price looks too low to be believable, it might not be a bargain at all. A computer-supply business can be set up in someone's living room. You might place an order in good faith, pay up front, and then find out that they are out of stock, their credit line with manufacturers is not sound, or they're about to go out of business. You risk not getting your supplies and not seeing your money again. Try to find a reasonably reliable mail-order house, even if it's across the country, and deal with them rather than buying ribbons, disks, and so forth at the computer store.

Some printers stand up better than others. Few users have had problems with an Epson printer. Printers do break, however, and when that happens you realize how much you depend on them. The single most likely part to break down is the print head. If your print head breaks down, you can be back in business soon because they wear out so regularly that they are

Tip 25:

Buying Paper

Don't buy paper through the mail. It's too heavy; anything you save on the base price you pay in shipping costs. Forms houses will sell you paper by the carton for $25 for a 3,000-sheet box of tractor-feed paper.

Tip 26:

Buying a Printer

Don't choose a particular printer because you can get the ribbons or some add-on cheaply.

carried in stock at service centers and even by some dealers.

There are also electronic failures. Few people realize how sophisticated an electronic device the printer has become. The Toshiba 1351 has 244K of memory and an 8086 on board: it's a computer in its own right. Like print heads, boards and electronics are readily available. Things such as motor shims and stepper motors usually don't break, however, so when they do it's rare to find someone who has the part in stock. They have to be specially ordered from the manufacturer, and that can mean weeks or months of waiting.

In general, those who are closest to the questions of printer service say that two-thirds of the problems they see are electronic and only one-third are mechanical. They also say that most electronic problems happen sooner rather than later. Most such problems are failures of the quality control systems at the manufacturer. That fact argues strongly for torture testing your printer (and the rest of the system, for that matter).

If you are fortunate, the store where you buy your next printer will run a burn-in test on your printer before they sell it to you. Not just the diagnostic test that comes with the machine, but a test that includes running the printer for an hour or so and covers all the printer features.

Most printers are surprisingly reliable, however, unless you're dealing with an off-the-wall brand name. You can usually identify them by their low list prices. Notice that we said low *list* prices, not low prices. A $379 letter-quality printer is not going to last well. Some low-priced machines are made not even of good plastic but of the cheapest available. They'll work fine for a year or so, but won't live long after that. Sad to say, more American than Japanese printers are problems.

As one dealer put it, "The Toshiba is the Rolls Royce of dot matrix printers; Epson, Okidata, and Star printers are the Plymouths, Fords, and Chevys."

Printer Peripherals

There are few things more frustrating than being seated at the keyboard of a $4,000 or $5,000 machine, unable to do any work on it because it is running a printing job.

Your computer is capable of reading a 25,000- or 30,000-character file into memory in 25 to 30 seconds. Your printer, however, is able to print only 30 characters per second if it is a fast letter-quality printer or 200 characters per second if it is a fast dot matrix printer. Thus, printing a 30,000-character document at 30 characters per second takes almost twenty minutes. If you print a high-speed draft, you tie up the machine for only two or three minutes, but even that short a time seems like an eternity when you are sitting in front of the machine.

The IBM DOS diskettes contain at least one program, PRINT.COM, that enables you to use the computer while printing a document, but if you try that, you'll find that your word processor runs slower than it did before the printing began.

Print spooling, however, allows you to read a document into an area of memory that's been set aside to hold it. Once the document is in the reserved area, called a *buffer,* the software returns control of the rest of the system to the user and begins feeding the characters in the buffer to the printer.

Print spooling is one reason for buying a multifunction expansion board for your system, because many of these boards provide spooling capability. Unfortunately, spoolers don't work with all software, so sometimes an in-line buffer is better, because it's totally transparent to most software.

An in-line buffer is an electronic device that lives between your computer and printer. The computer thinks the buffer is the printer, and the printer thinks the buffer is the computer. When you order a document printed, the computer sends it to the buffer, which takes the characters nearly as fast as the computer can send them. The computer sees the characters go and believes that the printer has finished. The characters are stored in the buffer and forwarded to the printer at a rate the printer can handle. The result of this process is that the control of the computer is returned to you as soon as the buffer finishes receiving the document, and you can resume work while printing continues.

In a business environment an in-line buffer is not a luxury. It frees the machine for more productive work. In fact, some buffers allow you to turn off the computer at the end of the day and still continue printing.

Business environments also often use soundproof boxes with daisy wheel printers, but the need for them is shrinking every day. In response to customer complaints about noise, manufacturers are bringing new machines to market that are not as noisy as the older ones were. Look beneath the lids of recently manufactured daisy wheel printers and you'll find insulated boxes and quieter mechanisms.

Tip 27:

Buffer Standards

The principle of the buffer sounds simple enough, but you should understand that there are virtually *no* standards for such devices, and getting them to communicate properly with both your computer and your printer may not always be easy.

The ABCs of Printing

As you've learned, computers have a set of terms all their own. Printer jargon is a dialect of computerese, a hybrid tongue that draws from electronics and from the printing industry.

For example, what is *microjustification?* Microjustified text is text that has been spaced so that the right margins of each page are even. To create that kind of spacing, a word-processing program puts a whole space here, a quarter of a space there, and so forth, until the line is finished and there aren't too many words that are spaced too widely apart.

Proportional spacing means that each character printed has a different width. That's easy for a printer to do, because the printer usually handles motion per letter internally when you set it for proportional spacing.

It's extremely difficult, however, to produce justified text that is proportionally spaced. That's largely because word-processing software does not control the motion of the print head. The word processor assumes that it's sending, say, 10 characters per inch to the printer and that every time 10 characters have been sent, the print head has moved one inch. If you are using proportional spacing, the printer adjusts the spaces between the letters and may be using slightly more or less than 10 characters per inch. Only about 25 or 30 percent of the word processors on the market support proportional spacing. Even fewer can handle proportionally spaced, justified text. For a word processor to do that, it must have a table of letter thicknesses built in. Then when the printer prints a *J,* the word processor knows that the print head has moved the width of a *J* and can adjust the end of the line accordingly.

Figures 3–3, 3–4, 3–5, 3–6, and 3–7 illustrate some of the basic fonts and type sizes that are available in most standard dot matrix printers. In some instances we have mixed bold, italic, and roman type faces to give you some idea of the flexibility that is possible. These figures were produced using PCWrite and an Epson FX 80 printer.

Tip 28:

Reassigning the Printer Port

If you've added a memory board that has a printer port, and you cannot seem to get your printer to work, try reassigning the printer, either with AS-SIGN (in DOS) or with a program that comes with the board (QSWAP with the Quadram board, for example). The printer default is LPT1, but you may need to ASSIGN LPT2. (A quick test is to type DIR >PRN. If the directory of the disk in the current drive doesn't appear on the printer, try reassigning the port.)

Figure 3–3 is printed in justified format using a pica, or 10-character-per-inch, typeface. Figure 3–4 is ragged-right using an elite, or 12-character-per-inch, typeface. The term "SOFT-WARE ROT" is printed in bold, and the citation is italicized bold. Figure 3–5 is proportionally spaced. Notice that the letters *i* and *I* require less space than, say, *g, s, r, c,* or *o.* Figure 3–6 is printed in compressed type (17 characters per inch).

Zero, the non-number which is perhaps the most important number of all for higher mathematics and cosmic calculations, was known among ancient races only to the Hindus of India and the Maya of the Americas, on opposite sides of the earth. There are indications that the Babylonians and the Chinese also once knew about zero, but forgot it.

Charles Berlitz, Native Tongues

Figure 3-3: Justified Pica Output

SOFTWARE ROT n. A hypothetical disease, the existence of which has been deduced from the observation that unused programs or features will stop working after sufficient time has passed, even if "nothing has changed." Also known as "bit decay."

from the *Stanford and MIT Artificial Intelligence Laboratories' unofficial glossary file*

Figure 3-4: Ragged-right Elite Output

English written signs sometimes give contradictory impressions to non-English-speakers. French visitors wonder at the sign "Sale" over a display of merchandise in shop windows, because *sale* means "dirty" in French.

Charles Berlitz, Native Tongues

Figure 3-5: Proportionally Spaced Output

Here is Edward Bear, coming downstairs now, bump,
.bump, bump, on the back of his head, behind
Christopher Robin. It is, as far as he knows the
only way of coming downstairs, but sometimes he
feels that there really is another way, if only
he could stop bumping for a moment and think of
it.

A. A. Milne

Figure 3-6: Compressed
Output (17 Characters per
Inch)

Finally, figure 3–7 illustrates some of the
special features that are available on many
printers.

This line is printed IN BOLD FACE

This line is printed IN COMPRESSED TYPE

This is a DOUBLE WIDTH line

This line is printed in ELITE

This line is printed in PICA

This is   SUPERSCRIPT

This line is printed in ITALIC

This is SUBSCRIPT

T̸h̸i̸s̸/l̸i̸n̸e̸/i̸s̸/p̸r̸i̸n̸t̸e̸d̸/i̸n OVERSTRIKE MODE/

This line is printed in TWO PASS PICA

This line is printed in TWO PASS ELITE

This line is printed in SECOND STRIKE

This line is printed with UNDERLINING

This line is printed with VARIABLE PITCH

Figure 3-7: Special Printing Features

4/The Operating System

Our little systems have their day.

Tennyson, *In Memoriam*

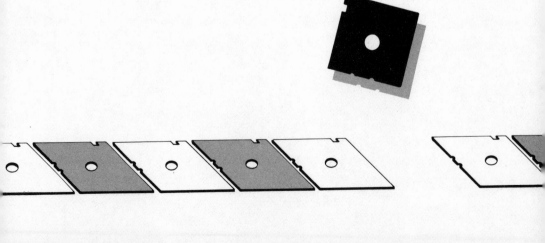

If a machine can be said to have a personality, then that personality is more deeply grounded in the operating system than in the hardware. It is the most important program that the computer uses, and the one that most users know least about.

The operating system of the PC is worth a book or two in itself. We won't claim completeness: all we want to do is to give you enough of a sampling of useful DOS commands to make you feel a bit more comfortable with DOS. As we go along, you should pick up one or two ideas that you can adapt to your own purposes. The discussion will be appropriate for DOS 2.0 and up. DOS 3.0 and 3.1 will be specified when necessary.

The operating system of a computer is a set of programs that manages the movement of information in the machine. The accomplishment of even the simplest tasks involves an impressive sequence of steps. Among other things, the programs in the operating system read the characters you type at the keyboard, manage the display of information on the screen, send that display to the printer or a modem, store that display on a diskette, or process commands that other programs send it—such as when you tell 1-2-3 or WordStar to retrieve a file, for example.

The first part of the operating system, ROM-BIOS (for Read Only Memory-Basic Input Output System) is a program that is etched permanently on a chip. Whenever the power switch is turned on, ROM-BIOS is activated. There's just enough information in ROM-BIOS to get the machine going and to position the read-write heads of drive A on side 0, track 0, sector 1 of the diskette. At that point, control is passed to the diskette. In a sense, ROM-BIOS is a part of the machine rather than of the operating system.

The first sector of every formatted diskette contains the *boot record,* another small program containing only enough information to get the system started. That program is the "bootstrap" by which the system pulls itself up. Most computers must have a boot record; therefore, you don't start computers, you "boot" them, and to restart a computer without first turning off the power, you "reboot" it.

The remainder of the operating system for the IBM comprises three main programs—the disk directory, the file allocation table, and an assortment of smaller programs. The three main parts of MS-DOS are the IBMBIO.COM (BIO for basic input/output again—an elaboration of ROM-BIOS); IBMDOS.COM, for disk operating system; and COMMAND.COM, the command processor.

Whenever you issue the DIRectory command for a disk that contains the file COMMAND.COM, that file will appear in the list of files on the disk. IBMBIO.COM and IBMDOS.COM are hidden and so will not appear in the list even if they are on the disk. However, both must be on a disk in order for the computer to recognize it as a system disk and to use it to boot the system. What's more, if they are not on a disk and other files have been copied to the disk, you cannot transfer IBMBIO.COM and IBMDOS.COM to the disk and expect the system to recognize it as a system disk. That's because IBMBIO.COM and IBMDOS.COM must be the first two files on the disk after the directory and file allocation table (see below).

Tip 29:

Different DOS Versions

I accidentally loaded DOS 1.1 and "lost" all the files in my directories. Reloading DOS 2.0 allowed them to reappear.

Each succeeding version of DOS, from 1.0 to 3.0, has contained a few more commands. Generally, it's to your advantage to use the latest version of DOS. Some DOS 2.x commands have been improved upon substantially in DOS 3.0, and some useful ones have been added. For example, DOS 3.0 includes drivers that support French, German, Italian, British, and Spanish keyboards and European date and currency formats.

DOS 3.0 also allows you to make files *read only*, which means that anyone can use these files, but they cannot be altered on the disk. If you are developing form letters, a data base, or spreadsheet models that will be used by many persons, the ability to create a read-only file is invaluable, because it can help prevent an unwary user from altering, and thus destroying, the underlying file.

With DOS 3.0, you also gain an external command—VDISK.SYS—that allows you to install as many as sixteen RAM disks. (See below for more on RAM disks.) One major improvement in DOS 3.0 is that if you happen to be deep in a subdirectory and want to execute an external command, all you have to do is give the name of the directory and the file that will be affected by that command; the operating system will find that file and execute the specified command. In DOS 2.0, it is necessary for you to be on the same directory level as the affected file in order to execute an external command.

In short, there's basically no good reason for not switching to DOS 3.0 or 3.1.

Generally, unless you are programming, your interest in DOS will be largely restricted to those commands that can help you organize your work. Even if you are programming, it will probably be a while before you have to concern yourself with DOS in any but the most superficial way. The majority of users employ DOS to manipulate files in some manner.

Tip 30:

The Learning Curve

How has the computer fallen short of my expectations? It's sometimes debatable as to whether I'm saving time.

In and Out of DOS

DOS commands are either internal or external. Internal commands are a part of the command processor, COMMAND.COM. With one exception, you cannot operate your PC unless you have loaded the command processor. (The exception is when you have turned on the power without a diskette in drive A. In that case, the machine loads a program called Cassette BASIC, and all you can do is write and run BASIC programs from a cassette. We will not discuss Cassette BASIC, on the assumption that you are using a system with at least one disk drive.)

Whenever you are not using an application program or a programming language, you are said to be at the command, DOS, or system level. When you are at command level and issue a command, it is passed first to COMMAND.COM. COMMAND.COM contains a list of commands, through which it searches for the command you issued. If your command is in the list (which is another way of saying it is an internal command), control of the system is transferred to that part of the COM-

Table 4-1: Internal DOS commands. The internal commands in DOS 2.x and 3.0 are the same. Asterisks indicate the commands discussed in chapter 4.

On-screen File Management Commands	Directory Management Commands
RENAME or REN	CD or CHDIR*
ERASE or DEL	MD or MKDIR*
TYPE*	RD or RMDIR*
COPY*	
VERIFY	

Device-oriented Commands	General Informational Commands
PROMPT	DATE
PATH*	TIME
EXIT	VERsion
CTTY	VOL
CLS	SET
BREAK	

Batch File Commands

ECHO*	GOTO
SHIFT	IF
FOR	PAUSE
REM	ERRORLEVEL
EXIST	

MAND.COM file that contains the instructions that must be executed.

The internal commands in DOS 3.0 are the same as in DOS 2.x. Table 4–1 shows them organized roughly according to the functions for which they are used.

External DOS commands are programs stored on the DOS diskette. Because external DOS commands are not part of any of the files that run when you boot the system, you have to make sure the files containing these commands are in a drive when you issue one such command.

Table 4–2 shows the directory of the DOS diskette and the files that are called when you issue a DOS command. Actually, when you issue the command, the system reads what you have typed on the keyboard, and if it cannot find the command in the command processor, it begins looking for files that correspond to what you have typed. For example, whenever you

Table 4-2: External DOS Commands. The underlined commands have been added in DOS 3.0. Asterisks indicate the commands discussed in chapter 4.

Commands

ANSI	BACKUP
FORMAT*	RESTORE
CHKDSK	PRINT
SYS	RECOVER
DISKCOPY	ASSIGN
DISKCOMP	TREE
COMP	GRAPHICS
EDLIN	SORT*
MODE	FIND
FDISK	MORE*
SHARE	ATTRIB
VDISK *	LABEL *
KEYBSP	KEYBIT
KEYBGR	KEYBUK
KEYBFR	SELECT
GRAFTABL	

want to make a new disk ready for use in your machine you must format it. To do that you have to issue the DOS command FORMAT. When you do, the system searches for a file called FORMAT.COM, FORMAT.EXE, or FORMAT.BAT. (They are searched in that order.) As soon as it finds the file, it reads it and executes the instructions that it finds.

Most new users get as far as the FORMAT and DIR commands in DOS and then plunge into their word processor, data base, spreadsheet, or whatever other applications they bought with their microcomputers. Sooner or later, they pick up such things as DISKCOPY (which you should usually avoid—see chapter 2), RENAME, DEL or ERASE, and COPY.

The Erased File (Forgotten But Not Gone)

In a story in the *New York Times,* late in 1984, a schoolteacher was quoted as saying that the alibi of the 80s had changed from "the dog ate my homework" to "the computer erased my disk." The well-prepared teacher only has to say: "That's okay, just give me the disk and tell me the name of the file."

Unless you are one of those rare people who never make a mistake, you will sooner or later press the Return key just a fraction of a second before you realize that you have told the machine to erase a file that you need desperately. When that happens, it is far from the disaster that it seems.

If the file is small enough, you may be able to retrieve it with DEBUG, a program that comes with your DOS diskettes and that may be used to rewrite parts of larger programs or even to write small assembly language programs. Several magazines have carried brief articles that purport to illustrate the use of DEBUG commands to retrieve an erased file. Using DEBUG this way is risky: it requires you to make changes in the file allocation table (FAT), and if you make one or two slips there, you may make other files inaccessible. You really should own some sort of program, such as the one in The Norton Utilities, that is designed to recover erased files.

To understand the process of recovering a lost file, you must know some of the simpler details of the directory and the FAT. The FAT consists of four sectors: the first and third are identical, as are the second and fourth. That duplication is a form of insurance, because if one of the FAT sectors is damaged, there will be a record in its twin. Whenever you save a file, its directory entry contains the name, file size, certain other attributes of the file, and—most important—the location of the first FAT entry about the file. In the FAT itself, the first entry gives the address of the first sector where the file is stored and the location of the next FAT entry about the file. When you want to use a file, the system finds the first link in the chain when it reads the directory and is conducted from there to the FAT.

The important thing to understand about the process of erasing a file is that the file is not actually erased. Two things happen when you ERASE (or DELete) a file: the first character of its name is changed to ASCII 229 in the directory and certain values in the FAT are set to zero. This explains why it takes so much less time to erase a file than to save it. When you save a file all the data it contains must actually be written on the disk.

When you do a DIR, the command processor reads the directory of the disk and displays all file names that begin with a valid character. If a file name begins with ASCII 229, the file does not appear in the directory listing. The FAT shows that space is available, and the next file you save may use some of the same sectors that were used by the file you erased.

Tip 31:

Precise Punctuation

Accept that you have to do it the computer's way. I'm learning that commas, colons, and semicolons are very important.

If you do not save any other files, however, the erased file remains on the disk, undisturbed. If you erase a file and then realize that you need it, do not save any files before using a program to unerase the file. If you have saved a file since erasing the file you need, you may still be able to recover part of the file, depending on the size of the file or files you saved after the erasure. If the newly saved files would have used fewer sectors than the erased file used, you may be partly in luck.

Because of the changes that take place in the FAT, restoring the file is not simply a matter of changing the first character of the name that remains in the directory. Consequently, beware of any suggestions that all you have to do is use DEBUG and fix one or two addresses in the directory. You also have to reallocate space in the FAT, and that's not generally easy to do.

DIR Revisited

DIR, one of the simplest of the DOS commands, is often substantially underutilized by the newcomer. Reading the user's guide that is included with the DOS manual gives the impression that there's only one way to use DIR. The manual itself contains more details about DIR, but by the time most people get there, they skip over DIR on the assumption that they've used it so often there's little or nothing left to learn. Not so.

The next time you use DIR, type:

DIR /W

Instead of the usual layout, which looks like this (files are those on the DOS 2.1 Supplemental Programs disk):

Volume in drive B has no label
  Directory of B:

EXE2BIN   EXE   1664   10–20–83 12:00p

LINK	EXE	39936	10–20–83	12:00p
DEBUG	COM	11904	10–20–83	12:00p
SAMPLES	BAS	3067	10–20–83	12:00p
ART	BAS	1920	10–20–83	12:00p
MUSIC	BAS	10291	10–20–83	12:00p
MUSICA	BAS	15072	10–20–83	12:00p
MORTGAGE	BAS	6272	10–20–83	12:00p
COLORBAR	BAS	1536	10–20–83	12:00p
DONKEY	BAS	3584	10–20–83	12:00p
CIRCLE	BAS	1664	10–20–83	12:00p
PIECHART	BAS	2304	10–20–83	12:00p
SPACE	BAS	1920	10–20–83	12:00p
BALL	BAS	2048	10–20–83	12:00p
COMM	BAS	4352	10–20–83	12:00p

             15 File(s)   69120 bytes free

you'll see this:

Volume in drive B has no label
  Directory of B:

EXE2BIN	EXE	LINK	EXE	DEBUG	COM	SAMPLES	BAS	ART	BAS
MUSIC	BAS	MUSICA	BAS	MORTGAGE	BAS	COLORBAR	BAS	DONKEY	BAS
CIRCLE	BAS	PIECHART	BAS	SPACE	BAS	BALL	BAS	COMM	BAS

  15 File(s)   69120 bytes free

The addition of /W to the command produces a wider display of files, with five files on each line. Using this command, when your disks contain more than 23 files, you can display all of them on the screen at the same time. Thus, if you need to compare the directories of two different disks, you can display a wide directory for the first and then call up the directory for the other drive, perhaps also with /W, without scrolling the directory of the first drive out of sight.

If you want to keep the date and time information on the screen, you can add /P to the DIR command, which prevents the directory list from scrolling off the top of the screen until you permit it.

Tip 32:

Naming Files

You should pick some firm convention for naming your files and stick with it. One of the surprising things to the newcomer is that files should probably be given names that are similar, but still distinctly different. New users often give files names that are as much unlike other names as possible. Although that makes them distinctive and easily recognizable, it also makes them awkward to use with wild-card characters. When you are performing some DOS operations (DIR or COPY but not TYPE, for example), you can insert a question mark in a file name and the command processor will read it as meaning that any single character can occupy the position of the question mark. If you use an asterisk, it will be interpreted to mean that one or more characters may occupy the remainder of the name. If you name your files carefully, you should be able to find files quite easily, even on crowded disks.

Not My TYPE

The TYPE command can be largely ignored. It suffers from poor design and makes users suffer with it. The main problem is that it simply dumps the contents of a file on the screen so fast that you cannot possibly read them. If you want to look at the file, you must type Ctrl S or Ctrl Num Lock to stop the screen and Ctrl S again to resume that mad scroll into oblivion. An external command, called MORE, is far better.

Throughout this book, whenever you see the term "file_name," as shown in Tip 33, use the name of a real file, either one that you have created for the purpose of testing something or one that already exists.

Three external DOS commands—MORE, SORT, and FIND—are called *filters*. That means they take data from other files or programs and manipulate it somehow. SORT and FIND do what you'd expect them to do: they sort and find. We'll look at them in a moment.

MORE is a useful command, but it has a serious drawback for the unwary or careless. To see how it works and how it can get you in trouble, find a sizable (10–12K) file that you won't mind losing and copy it onto the same disk with the MORE.COM file. Now TYPE the file. As usual, once the file begins scrolling up the screen, you must use Ctrl Num Lock or Ctrl S if you want to read it. Now type

MORE <file_name

This time, rather than scrolling unhindered off the top of the screen, the scrolling should have stopped the moment that the screen was full. At the bottom of the screen, you should have seen the line

—More—

Pressing any key causes the screen to scroll again until another screen full of data is displayed.

What can go wrong with such a simple command? To see, type the following (notice that the greater-than symbol is used here instead of the less-than symbol that should be used):

MORE >file_name

Nothing appears to happen. You don't get a screen full of data; you don't get anything. In order to regain control of the keyboard, you have to type Ctrl Break or Ctrl C (hold down the Ctrl key and press either the Break key or the *C* key). That returns you to the system

Filters and Pipes

Tip 33:

A Use for TYPE

What use is TYPE, then? One useful thing it does is to allow you to send a file directly to the printer with no waiting whatsoever. To try this, pick out a small file, one you are willing to waste a bit of paper on, and issue the command

TYPE file_name >prn

Tip 34:

The Unperceptive Computer

The trouble with computers, a frustrated programmer said, is that they do what you tell them to do, not what you want them to do.

prompt. Now do a DIR and see how big your file is. It should be around two bytes long. If you TYPE it, you'll see that it's empty (the two bytes are just the beginning- and end-of-file markers, which do not appear on the screen when you TYPE a file).

So, all you did was mistype a single character and you erased a file.

The section on page 71 on batch files shows you a simple way to avoid the problem altogether, but for the moment let's look at what you just did a little more carefully. The only difference between successfully using MORE and erasing a file was in how the symbols "<" and ">" were used. You can think of those symbols as arrows pointing in the direction that information will flow in a command. Therefore, the command MORE <file_name tells the machine that the information in the file with the specified name should be funneled into the command MORE. When that's done, you get the results you were looking for.

Conversely, when you give the command MORE >file_name, you tell the machine to take the results of executing the command MORE and funnel them into a file called file_name. Because nothing is directed into the MORE command, nothing comes out, and that's exactly what the machine stores in the specified file—nothing. Except for two bytes, the file is empty. There already is a file called file_name, but the machine assumes that you know what you want and writes over the old version with the new one.

The concept just discussed involves the redirection of input and output. MORE, SORT, and FIND are examples of how DOS takes data and redirects it. Data can be directed into a file, to the screen, or to the printer. If you have ever used the command

COPY CON:file_name

you have redirected output from the console to a file. Similarly, if you enter the command

TYPE file_name >PRN

you redirect output from the console to the printer. Finally, if you type

DIR >NUL

the busy light of the drive will go on, but nothing will seem to have happened. You have just redirected the DIRectory listing from the screen to the device NUL.

Remember, the commands in DOS are programs; they are stored as files and must have some kind of data to work with. That data is input that you supply or that you direct the system to supply. One program can feed information into another and send the results to wherever you indicate. You determine the direction of the movement of data by your use of ">" and "<."

You've just seen that you can create a file or rewrite an existing file by using ">." However, if you simply type

>file_name

following the system prompt in DOS, nothing will happen. The disk drive will whirl a bit, but you won't even get an error message. If you type

DIR >DIRLIST

the drive will turn on and run a bit before the system prompt returns. If you then type DIR, you will see the file DIRLIST in your directory. Type the command TYPE DIRLIST and you will see the directory that did not appear on the screen a moment ago.

Now type

SORT <DIRLIST

The directory listing contained in DIRLIST

will appear on the screen in ascending alphabetic order. To reverse the order, type the command using the /R option (that is, SORT /R <DIRLIST). The SORT filter will also take a numerical option that enables you to sort a file based on a particular column in which some element begins. For example, in a directory listing, the date on which a file was created always begins in column 22, so the command

$$\text{SORT } /+22 \text{ <DIRLIST}$$

will produce a listing sorted by date with the earliest date first. (Notice that you must supply a forward slash, a plus sign, and a number before you give the name of the file.) If you want to sort the file so that the latest date comes first, you would use

$$\text{SORT } /R /+22 \text{ <DIRLIST}$$

To sort by file size use "/+14"; by date, "/+22"; and by time, "/+32".

To save the results of a sort, you can issue the command with the ">" symbol to write a new file. That is, type

$$\text{SORT <DIRLIST >DIRSORT}$$

Don't use the same file name for input and output. Doing so creates an odd situation, because the system must create a file to which it will write the new version of the list, but it must take the data to be sorted out of a file with the same name. How can it know which file to use? Somehow DOS does manage to deal with the problem, but if you do use the same name for input and output and then TYPE the file to the screen, you'll see that about halfway through the final version of the file there is a string of strange characters in place of some of the information in the file.

Tip 35:

Sort and Compare Directories

Suppose you want to sort and compare two directories, one from the disk in drive A and one from the disk in drive B. Because using the command >file_name writes over files, you would think that it would be necessary to give them two different names. It isn't, however. Rather than using two files, you can write the sorted directories to the same file, specifying that one of them be appended to the end of the other. All you have to do is use ">>" when you give the name of the file to which you want the output of the sort to be directed. That is, you would type

SORT <DIRLISTA >DIRSORT

SORT <DIRLISTB >>DIRSORT

These commands would enable you to compare two or more disks for duplicate files or to find the most recent version of a file on several disks without having to make notes as the information scrolls on the screen.

Suppose that you've created a file called DIRSORT and it contains the directory entries of half a dozen disks. For some reason, you want to locate all the files on those disks that were created on a particular day—say, September 9, 1984 (that was a Sunday, and you want to know why you spent the day working, rather than playing golf, painting the kitchen, or napping). You can use the FIND filter for that.

Like that of SORT, the output of the FIND command can be redirected to a file. FIND locates all instances of lines containing the string (sequence of characters) for which you are searching. It sends those instances to

the screen, to a printer ("">PRN""), or to a file
("">"" or "">>file_name""). In short, except that
it requires you to provide the string to look for,
FIND behaves like SORT. There are three options of the FIND filter that enable you to locate lines that do *not* contain the string (""/V""),
to count the lines containing the string but not
to display them (""/C""), or to have the FIND
command tell you the number of the line it has
copied from the file (""/N"").

To locate the names of the files you created
that Sunday, you would type

FIND /N ""09-09-84"" <DIRSORT
>SUNDAY

Tip 36:

Limits of SORT and FIND

SORT and FIND are
handy to have around the
operating system and
make the PC a more use-
ful tool, even without
many application pro-
grams. If you do a lot of
searching and selecting
from many files, however,
don't expect too much of
these programs. They are
good, but they are no
match for a file manager
and they certainly
shouldn't be asked to substitute for a data base
management system like
dBase II, Power-base, or
one of the other full-scale
programs.

Although making files and experimenting
with them can help you learn how commands
work, when you are actually working on the
computer, those files can begin littering the
workspace on your disks. In fact, it isn't necessary to create an intermediate file when you are
using SORT or FIND. Using what DOS calls a
pipe, you can feed the output from one command directly into another. To do that you use
the key marked "" | "". (It's next to your left little
finger as you reach for the shift key.) If you
tried to redirect output to the SORT command
using the command DIR >SORT, you would
wind up with a file called SORT (fortunately,
you would not harm the SORT command because that runs from a file called SORT.EXE).
So, to distinguish between redirecting the output of a command to a file and redirecting it to
another command, DOS uses "" | "". The simplest
and quickest way to see piping at work is to
type

DIR | SORT

You can also pipe the output from DIR to
SORT and then redirect SORT's output to a

file, as was shown above. Just type

DIR ¦SORT >file_name

Keeping track of things is always a chore. If you don't do it regularly and consistently, you can lose control. Unlike paper files, the information in disk files is not instantly available to you the moment you glance at it. You must label your disks and periodically relabel them.

Batch Commands and Batch Files

In a sense, a batch file is a program. A program is simply a file containing a series of statements that, when read by the processor, are understood as commands and are executed by the system. The statements could be in BASIC, C, or assembly language. In a batch file, the statements are DOS commands such as DIR, COPY, or FORMAT. There are also some special commands that are used only in batch files: FOR, REM, ECHO, GOTO, IF, PAUSE, and SHIFT.

A batch file may contain both internal and external DOS commands issued; these commands will be executed in sequence without your having to intervene. If you find that you are often performing the same tasks again and again, it probably will pay you to create batch files containing the command sequences you use repeatedly. Then you'll be able to type a single word, or perhaps a line, and let the system take over the remaining work.

The most common batch file that people use is one that is executed when the system is turned on; this file is called an AUTOEXEC batch file. Every time you turn the power on, the system runs through its diagnostics and then looks for several kinds of files. If those files exist, the system reads them and carries out the instructions they contain. If the system finds a file called AUTOEXEC.BAT (the .bat suffix identifies batch files), it will read each line in the file as though it had just been typed on the keyboard.

For example, a batch file could be used to make sure that a typo in the MORE command line will not erase a file (see the discussion of MORE above). The first thing you need to know is that changing the names of files on the DOS diskettes doesn't affect their operation, in most cases. If you change the name of MORE.COM to LOOK.COM, for example, it still works correctly when you type LOOK <file_name.

The second thing you need to know is that you can use string variables (called *dummy parameters* in the DOS manual) in a batch file. (A string is a character or sequence of characters that is read as characters, not as numbers or formulas. The names "Beth" and "David" are strings. "A + B" can also be a string, if you don't want a solution to the implied problem; it can also be a formula, the answer to which is a numeric variable.) String variables operate as regular numeric variables do; they are used to represent unspecified strings and may be replaced by any other strings. The variables will be replaced by the names of the files that you want the batch file to manipulate. You can include as many as ten such variables in a batch file.

A string variable is identified in a batch file by a percentage symbol followed by a number. Thus, %1 is the first string that the batch file will read from the command line you type; %2 is the second, and so forth, up to ten such variables.

The problem with the MORE command would be solved if it were possible to use the command without having to use the "<" symbol at all. To do that, all you have to do is change the name of the MORE.COM file to something else and create a batch file that uses that new file name that includes a variable so that you can type only the word MORE and the name of the file, separated by a single space.

First, change the name of the file MORE.COM to LOOK.COM by using the REName command. Type

REN MORE.COM LOOK.COM

Now, without leaving DOS, type

COPY CON:MORE.BAT
LOOK <%1
Ctrl Z (or F6)

Next, pick out some file name to replace the variable %1 and type

MORE file_name

You get the same result as if you had typed MORE<file_name, but with no possibility of erasing anything. Typing MORE now causes the system to search for a batch file called MORE.BAT (instead of the DOS file called MORE.COM); MORE.BAT then finds the file called LOOK, which used to be called MORE.COM, and replaces the string variable %1 with the file name you supplied after the MORE command. The added time the system takes to find MORE.BAT is repaid by the integrity of your files.

Because the execution of a FORMAT command erases all the data on a disk, it can be dangerous. It is easy to erase a disk unintentionally, even a hard disk containing hundreds of files or fewer, but much larger, files. A batch-file approach similar to that above can be used to prevent erasing a hard disk by formatting it unintentionally. Type

REN FORMAT.COM INIT.COM

to change the name of the FORMAT.COM program file to INIT.COM.

Now type

```
COPY CON: FORMAT.BAT
ECHO OFF
IF %1= =c: GOTO CHANGE
IF %1= =C: GOTO CHANGE
INIT %1
IF NOT %1= =c: GOTO END
IF NOT %1= =C: GOTO END
:CHANGE
INIT B:
:END
CtrlZ (or F6)
```

This is a solution similar to the one we used with the problem of MORE.COM's weakness, but it adds a wrinkle or two. First, it uses the ECHO command. When ECHO is turned off, the remaining commands in the file do not appear on the screen. That is, they are not "echoed" to the screen. Second, it uses IF to check which drive you have tried to format. IF statements test a condition, and if it is true they execute the command that is on the same line. If the condition is not true, the system skips to the next line without executing the command in the IF statement. (Because the IF statement is case sensitive, and the formatting program is not, you must use two IFs to cover both upper- and lower-case cs). The IF statements use a GOTO command to send the system to the Label called CHANGE. Thus, if you type FORMAT C: (or c:), the batch file transfers control to the line following the label (labels must begin lines and must be preceded by a colon). In that case, the batch file overrides your command to format drive C with the command INIT B:, which invokes the formatting program (now called INIT.COM) and specifies drive B. In short, if you want to format drive C, you must type INIT C.

If you have not attempted to format drive

Tip 37:

Upgrade Your DOS

Here's another reason to use DOS 3.x: if you attempt to format a hard disk when you are using DOS 3.x, you are warned about what you are trying to do and given a chance to cancel the command.

Tip 38:

Hard Disk Wipeouts

To prevent a fixed disk wipeout, mask the FORMAT command, or set up a batch file to force the FORMAT to work only on the A: drive.

C, neither IF statement is true, so the command INIT %1 is executed. After the first disk is formatted, the system prompts you to format another. If you answer yes, the formatting program retains control of the system. If you answer no, however, the formatting program returns control of the system to the batch file, which resumes execution at the line following INIT %1. That, too, is an IF statement, but it tests for NOT C:. If this test were not in the file, the next command that would be executed after the formatting program returned control to the batch file would be the one following :CHANGE. The two IF NOT statements cause the batch file to skip the INIT B: command and return control of the system to you.

This batch file isn't the only way to solve this problem. Others would include using DEBUG to patch FORMAT.COM, or writing a BASIC or assembly language program to prevent erasing your hard disk.

On those occasions when you would like to compare the directories of two disks, try this:

COPY CON:COMPARE.BAT
DIR A: ┆SORT / +22 >DIRLIST
DIR B: ┆SORT / +22 >>DIRLIST
TYPE DIRLIST >PRN
CtrlZ (or F6)

Gradually, as your disks fill up, you might want to learn more about the use of directories. Unfortunately, IBM and Microsoft chose to organize the DOS manual alphabetically, so many commands that are used together wind up in the manual located at distances from each other. For example, the commands that deal with directories and the things that you can do to organize your work are PATH, DIR, TREE, MKDIR (MD), CHDIR (CD), and RMDIR

Tip 39:

A Batch LOGOUT

If you always work with RAM disks, you will want to make sure that you don't switch off the system before you've copied files from the RAM disk onto disks. A batch file called LOGOUT.BAT can attend to that. To suppress all the names of the files, you can construct the statements in the batch files so that you redirect output to >NUL. For example, the statement

COPY B:file_name
A:*.* >NUL

in a batch file (or directly from the keyboard) keeps the "1 File(s) copied" message from appearing on the screen.

Directories and Subdirectories

(RD). Although there is a short treatise on directories about 180 pages into the DOS manual, the details of the commands are all located in the second section of the manual.

The DOS manual gives the impression that directories are useful primarily if you have a hard disk. That isn't the case at all. Whether you use floppy or hard disks, you can use directories to get around one of the limitations of the operating system—a limitation that is really annoying if your work happens to call for a large number of small files.

The problem is that the operating system stores information about file locations in directory sectors, each of which can hold information about only 16 files. On a single-sided disk there are 4 directory sectors; on a double-sided disk there are seven. That means that single-sided disks can hold only 64 files and double-sided disks can hold 112. If you store many small files, you may find yourself in the aggravating position of seeing the message "File creation error," accompanied by the statement "0 File(s) copied" and the information that you still have 170,000 bytes free on the disk.

If you use directories, however, you can store as many files as the disk will hold, without running into the limit imposed by the number of directory sectors. Thus, if you have 200 1,500-byte files, you can fit them all on one double-sided disk.

Making and Using Directories

First, imagine you've formatted a disk with the volume name CORRESPOND and you're using it for both personal and business letters. To help you keep them all organized, you should make two subdirectories. Assume that you send far more business letters than personal ones. That suggests that you should have your business letters further organized into additional subdirectories, but that your personal letters can all be lumped together in a single subdirectory.

Figure 4–1 illustrates the concept of subdirectories. The DOS manual calls the base level of the disk's hierarchy the *root directory*. This figure, like diagrams that illustrate the directory structure, shows the root at the top (in this case, the root is Disk 1) and resembles an upside-down tree. All levels other than the root are considered subdirectories. That puts you in the strange position of going down the tree from the root. It helps, when you are typing the commands, to think of the backwards slash ("\") as though it were the word *down*. The tree metaphor changes in mid-thought, however, because what you would normally call *branches* on a tree are here called *paths* and have *path names*.

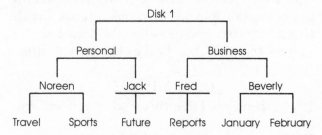

Figure 4-1: Sample Subdirectory Structure

The DOS command to create directories is MKDIR, which is abbreviated as MD. Load the disk and type

MD BUSINESS

MD PERSONAL

If you then type DIR, the screen that appears will look something like this:

Volume in drive B is CORRESPOND
  Directory of B:

BUSINESS	<DIR>	9–07–84	11:32a
PERSONAL	<DIR>	9–07–84	11:32a

  2 File(s) 360448 bytes free

Notice that the screen says you have made two files. If you were to tell the system to type those files, nothing would happen. DOS calls directory entries files because it has to keep track of them somehow.

One of the things that makes many people decide not to use directories is that at first it can be difficult to understand how to move around within them once you've set them up. The confusing part of working with directories is the use of the backslash. The easiest way to remember how to deal with it is that if you are moving *down* the same path, from one level to the next, moving only one level at a time, you do not need the backslash. If there is no backslash in a command, DOS searches for the specified directory or file at the current level. It is only when you are moving down more than a single level or moving from one directory path to another that you must use the backslash.

So, to use BUSINESS as the current directory, type

CD BUSINESS

If you then type DIR, this is what you will see:

Volume in drive B is CORRESPOND
  Directory of B:\BUSINESS

```
.            <DIR>    9-07-84   11:32a
. .          <DIR>    9-07-84   11:32a
   2 File(s)    360448 bytes free
```

The "Directory of B:" line tells you the path name of the current directory. If only a backslash appears after the colon in this line (as was the case in the preceding illustration), it means that the root is the current directory. This line also tells you how many levels you have moved from the root directory—by adding 1 to the number of backslashes in this line you can tell how many levels you must move up to reach the root directory.

You must open subdirectories one at a time. For example, if you are in the root directory you can create a subdirectory two levels away, but you must create the subdirectory in the middle first.

You can open subdirectories for each of the businesses with which you correspond. For example, using the MD command, you could create subdirectories called HERCULES, ATLAS, AJAX, and MINOS. Here's what the DIR command would produce after these subdirectories were created:

Volume in drive B is CORRESPOND
   Directory of B:\BUSINESS

.	<DIR>	9-07-84	11:32a
. .	<DIR>	9-07-84	11:32a
HERCULES	<DIR>	9-07-84	12:02p
ATLAS	<DIR>	9-07-84	12:02p
AJAX	<DIR>	9-07-84	12:03p
MINOS	<DIR>	9-07-84	12:04p

   6 File(s)   356352 bytes free

By typing

CD AJAX

You can move down to the AJAX subdirectory. But what if you want to move from AJAX to MINOS? One way to do that is to tell the operating system that you want to find the file named BUSINESS\MINOS (remember that DOS thinks of subdirectories as a kind of file). That is, you would type

CD \BUSINESS\MINOS

You can move from a third level directly to a second level by typing the backslash followed by the path name of the directory. For example, to move from BUSINESS\MINOS to BUSINESS, all you have to do is type

CD \BUSINESS

Directory Levels

One of the drawbacks of using directories is that you may be at the second or third level of a disk when you change the default drive. That does *not* change your directory level for the drive you are leaving. If you then copy files to the disk you just left, they will be in the directory from which you issued the command to change default drives. If that's where you want them, fine. If not, you will have to copy them to the correct directory and then delete them from the incorrect one. There is no command that copies a file to one directory and then deletes it from the original directory.

The more you have to type, however, the more likely you are to make errors. DOS provides a way to minimize such typing errors. If you were working on a letter in the MINOS subdirectory and wanted to look at a letter in the AJAX directory, you would not have to type the entire sequence of directory name and file name. To move up one level, you need only type the two dots that you see when you list a subdirectory's contents. Suppose, for example, that you are deep in the subdirectory BUSINESS\MINOS\OCT and you want to get quickly to BUSINESS\MINOS\SEPT to check a letter you sent last month. To do that, you need to return to the MINOS subdirectory and then move down to the SEPT subdirectory. You can use two dots to represent each level above to which you want to move, so all you have to type is

CD ..\SEPT

Similarly, if you wish to get to the ATLAS subdirectory, which is on the same level as the MI-

Programs and Path Names

Another drawback of using directories is that some programs do not support the use of directories and either will refuse to accept a full path name or will not display files in a subdirectory.

NOS subdirectory, you have to move up two levels, so you'd type:

CD ..\..\ATLAS\SEPT

Lastly, when you want to move directly to the root level, just type

CD\

No matter where you are, this command will return you to the root directory.

Up a TREE

Without the TREE command, using directories would be much more confusing, as files have a way of getting lost in unexpected branches. It's not unusual to run TREE on a disk you haven't used in a long time and turn up a few files that you were sure the machine swallowed. They'd merely been filed in places you never looked.

TREE is simple to use, because all you have to do is specify the disk drive. If you type TREE /F, the command will list the directories as well as the files. Sometimes, of course, the disk is so packed with files that a hard copy is more useful than having them display on the screen. You can send the display to the printer by typing

TREE /F B: >PRN

That command would send the complete directory structure to the printer. If you wish, you can store that directory as a file by substituting a file name for PRN.

The function keys, F1 through F5, provide one of the most often overlooked ways to make life easy when you are in DOS. Table 4–3, which is similar to the chart found on page "Keyboard 3–10" in your *Guide to Operations*, explains the use of function keys.

Tip 42:

Deleting Subdirectories

After a time, you accumulate a lot of unnecessary files and directories. Files can be deleted with DEL, but that doesn't work with subdirectories. To delete a subdirectory, you must first delete all of the files it contains and then delete the subdirectory itself with RMDIR.

Using Function Keys in DOS

Table 4-3: DOS Function Keys

Key	Function
F1	The screen redisplays the previously entered line, one character at a time.
F2	When F2 is pressed with a character, the screen redisplays the previously entered line up to the character entered.
F3	The screen redisplays the entire previously entered line.
F4	When F4 is pressed with a character, all of the characters in the previously entered line, up to the character entered, are deleted.
F5	Pressing this key stores the currently displayed line for further editing.

To see a few practical uses for these keys, first create a file by typing

DIR >DIRLIST

That will create a file called DIRLIST, into which the output of the DIR command will be directed. If you're using a disk without too many files, type

DIR >>DIRLIST

The output of the second DIR will be added to the bottom of the file that you created a moment earlier. Now press

F1

Each time you press it, another letter of the command you just issued will appear. You can get the same result by pressing the right arrow key. Rather than rewriting the file DIRLIST again, press

Ctrl C

to end the command. Now press F3. The entire command returns. Again, stop the command with Ctrl C and type

That should produce DIR >DIR, which you may finish any way you choose.

At one point in the development of the manuscript of this book, we learned that the files on one disk were in a sorry state. One file that was barely five sectors long was sprinkled around the disk in four unconnected pieces. Another much longer file was in about six pieces. This kind of disjointed storage typically happens when a disk is used often and contains a lot of files that change frequently. As the files grow, they cannot fit in the same space as they occupied previously, so DOS must put pieces of them in other tracks and sectors. In order to restore them to contiguous sectors and thereby speed up loading and saving, we copied a number of them from disk to disk. Being able to use the function keys extensively kept the job from being even more tedious than it sounds. All the files concerning spreadsheets, for example, were entitled ssnote$x$.txt, where x was a number. The first command we typed was

COPY B: \TEXT\SSNOTE1.TXT A:

The next was easy, because all we had to do for each file after the first was type F2, the number used in the last file, the next number, and F3. For example, the sequence used to go from SSNOTE1.TXT to SSNOTE2.TXT was

F2 1 2 F3

The sequence F2 1 produced B:\TEXT\ SSNOTE on the command line. Typing the 2 automatically overwrites the 1 that appeared in the original line. Pressing F3 yielded the rest of the line, .TXT A:. We could not have done it so easily if we had used file names that were more different from one another.

Buffers

Many programs perform frequent disk reads because they were originally designed to run on smaller systems than are available now. There are a couple of things you can do to lessen the number of disk reads a program makes, depending on your system.

The first option is to configure your system when you boot it. When you first power up an IBM PC, DOS looks for a CONFIG.SYS file. If it finds one, it executes any commands in that file before doing anything else. What you want to do is put a BUFFERS command in the file. A buffer is a part of RAM into which files are written. When the system looks for the file, it checks first to see whether any part of it has been put in a buffer. If so, it gets that part of the file from the buffer; if not, it goes to the disk. Buffers take up space in RAM, so the more buffers you create, the less space you'll have for data files. In addition, if you have too many buffers open, you may not see the disk whirring, but you won't gain any speed, because it may take the system longer to search all the buffers than it would to find something on a disk.

The system default setting is BUFF-ERS=2. You may want to start out with BUFFERS=20 and work up or down from there. The maximum is BUFFERS=99.

You can create a CONFIG.SYS file with WordStar or any other editor (EDLIN, for example). If you use WordStar, put the disk you normally use for booting the system into drive B (make sure it's not write-protected) and change the default drive to B. Open a document file called CONFIG.SYS and type the following line:

BUFFERS=20

Then save the file. DOS looks for a CON-FIG.SYS file only when you boot the system, so you won't notice any change in performance until the next time you boot it. If it's still reading the disk more than you'd like after the next boot, you can try increasing the number of buffers a bit more. Each buffer uses 528 bytes of RAM, so if you create 20 buffers you consume about 10K more of RAM than is used by the default setting. If your applications and utility programs are already pushing the limits of your system's capacity, increasing the number of buffers may not be a good move.

You can also use the COPY command in DOS to create the CONFIG.SYS file. To do so, with your boot disk in the active drive, type

COPY CON:CONFIG.SYS

When the underline cursor appears, type

BUFFERS = 20
CtrlZ (or F6)

That will save the file. The next time you boot the system, 20 buffers will be allocated. If you need to change the number of buffers or add other configuration commands to the file, you can edit it with EDLIN, WordStar, or your favorite editor.

RAM Disks

Another way to speed up programs that do a lot of disk reads and those that use a lot of overlays (parts of the program that are not loaded into memory until the user issues the commands they contain) is by using a RAM disk. The slowest operation in the computer is reading the disk. Data transfer for a file or program in RAM is three to four times faster than that for one read from a disk. Many multifunction cards contain software that enables you to set aside a part of RAM to be used as though it were a disk.

DOS 3.0 supports RAM disks with the VDISK.SYS program (for *virtual disk*, which is

RAM Disks

One disadvantage of RAM disks is that if the power fails, you lose any work you've done since the last time you saved a file on a disk or diskette. If you are going to use a RAM disk, you should save your work frequently.

another name for RAM disks, as is *disk emulator*). The advantage of using DOS 3.0's disk program is that you can set aside memory that is either on an expansion board or on the mother board. Some RAM disk programs restrict RAM disks to the expansion board. DOS 3.0's VDISK.SYS will also support as many as 16 RAM disks. Because the COMSPEC statement works in DOS 3.0 (it doesn't work the way you'd expect in DOS 2.x), you can set up one RAM disk, into which you copy COMMAND.COM and then from which COMMAND.COM is always invoked. If you already have an A drive and a B drive (which means that the RAM disk you are creating will be drive C), put the following statements in a CONFIG.SYS file:

    LASTDRIVE=C
    DEVICE=VDISK.SYS 24 512 16

The LASTDRIVE=C line establishes that you want only three drives—A and B, which you already have, and C, which you will create as a device in the next line. This statement could also be LASTDRIVE=D, LASTDRIVE=E, and so on, through LASTDRIVE=P. Thus, you can have as many as 16 drives.

The statement DEVICE=VDISK.SYS 24 512 16, calls the VDISK.SYS file and specifies that drive C will be a 24K drive that contains 512 byte sectors and has room for 16 directory entries. (Apparently 16 directory entries is the minimum—you can set the directory entries to 1, but the system changes it to 16.)

Now enter the following lines in your AUTOEXEC.BAT file:

    SET COMSPEC=C:\COMMAND.COM
    COPY COMMAND.COM C:

The COMSPEC option of the SET command

tells the system to look for the command processor in the drive you have specified (in this case, C). The command processor in DOS 3.0 is around 5K bytes larger than DOS 2.x, and you need a bit more space in the RAM disk for sector management and directory entries. Assigning 24K bytes to the drive should leave 512 bytes, or one full sector, for such use. That's close to the minimum that can be used, so you shouldn't write other files to the RAM disk.

Now, whenever you leave a program and return to the operating system, you don't have to have a copy of COMMAND.COM on the disk in drive A.

As mentioned above, each RAM disk you set up with DEVICE=VDISK.SYS in a CONFIG.SYS file is assigned a letter based on the physical drives your system contains. If you have three physical drives, the first VDISK.SYS in the file will become drive D, the second will become drive E, and so forth. If you have three physical drives (A, B, and C) and you set LASTDRIVE=G, then you can put only four DEVICE=VDISK.SYS lines in the batch file (D, E, F, and G).

One other point about RAM disks: if you are using large programs that must reside in RAM, adding a RAM disk may cramp your style. A word processor that remains resident can use as much as 60K or 70K of RAM, which will then be unavailable to other programs. Add a utility program, such as Sidekick or Spotlight, and you take up another 60K to 80K, for a total of 120K to 150K. Your 384K machine is now down to around 234K. Add a 64K RAM disk and you don't have enough space left to run Lotus 1-2-3.

That fact argues for more memory, and that's what makes owning (or using) a PC a lot like owning a boat—the machine is never quite big enough to do all you want to do with it.

Tip 44:

Always More Memory

Whether you want more memory or not, programs come out that do things you want but that demand more memory. Or you want to run some programs that can remain in RAM while other programs run, so you have to add memory.

5/Word Processing

Polonius: What do you read, my lord?
Hamlet: Words, words, words.

Shakespeare, *Hamlet*

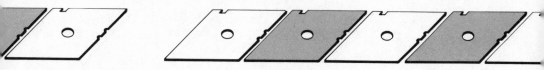

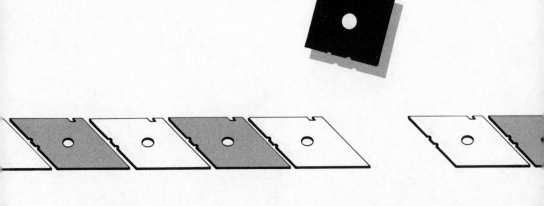

Of all the kinds of software available, none is used more widely than word-processing software. Even people whose work is dominated by number crunching use a word processor sooner or later to write a note, a letter, or a report. Nor does any other kind of software seem to consume as much users' time as word-processing programs do. BCS members surveyed for this book reported spending as much time using word processors as they did using data base and spreadsheet programs combined. Even when games, graphics, and communications were added to data base and spreadsheet programs, they still used word processors more than 40 percent of the time.

It isn't possible for this book to deal with every word-processing program a user can consider. The depth of the market seems to have drawn almost every software developer into the word-processing race. This chapter will look at some of the minimal features you should demand of a word-processing program if you need to produce more than an occasional note or letter (if your needs were that limited, you could squeak by using DOS). Word-processing software has developed some real muscle and some more friendly interfaces recently, so in addition to looking at the basics, this chapter will also look at some of the advanced features available in some programs. Finally, the chapter will discuss a few of the common problems people have when actually using word-processing software, especially those regarding moving word-processor files to other applications and moving files between one word processor and another.

If you are familiar with typewriters but new to microcomputers, you've probably noticed that microcomputer keyboards usually contain more keys than typewriters. In particular, you have

Word Processing on the PC

probably noticed the function keys (F1 through F10) at the left of the IBM keyboard and the Ctrl (for *Control*), Esc (for *Escape*), and Alt (for *Alternate*) keys, also on the left. Some word processors, such as Volkswriter, are primarily function-key driven, which means that they use keys F1–F10 to carry out a number of important commands. In contrast to a program that is driven by the function keys, some programs are command driven, meaning that you issue commands using Ctrl, Esc, or Alt keys in conjunction with letters on the normal typing part of the keyboard.

Most word-processing programs written specifically for the IBM PC use the function keys extensively. Older programs adapted to run on the IBM PC cling to their older command sequences, although later releases of the programs sometimes use the function keys in a limited way. Some programs use the function keys in conjunction with the shift, Alt, and Ctrl keys to amplify the set of commands.

All this is not to say that a command-driven word processor is inferior to one driven by function keys. The difference is largely a matter of taste. Some people just can't get used to typing such things as Ctrl Q F to do something, when typing F9 could do the same thing. Although the latter is clearly easier, it really doesn't require any more memorization than the former. One program may fit your needs and your sense of what is easy to use, while giving another person endless trouble and frustration. Although WordStar is the clear winner, year after year, of the word-processing sales sweepstakes, many users loathe it—many love it, too. Many people continue to use and to defend the excellence of WordStar only because they don't want to spend the time learning to use something else. In fact, there are several programs on the market that are easier to learn, easier to use, and as powerful and versatile as WordStar.

The difference between word-processing and text-editing programs should be mentioned here. There is a program on your DOS diskettes called EDLIN. EDLIN is a text editor, not a word processor. You can use it to process one line of text at a time. There are some text editors on the market that will allow you to deal with more than one line at a time, but that feature remains of little use to people who really want word processors.

A word-processing program should do at least three jobs: text editing, which means entering and changing text; text formatting, such as setting margins, paragraph indentation, and paragraph formation and reformation; and document printing, including sending codes to the printer to set line spacing, type size, and page numbers. A word-processing program might do all three jobs from within the program, or it may use separate modules for each job. If any one of those functions is missing, the program shouldn't be called a word processor.

Used with word-processing software, the microcomputer presents the new user with the most understandable of tasks in the most friendly manner. If you press the *q* key, a *q* appears on the screen, and if you then press *uick,* the computer gives you the word *quick.* So far that's exactly what a typewriter does. The superiority of a word processor is apparent, though, if you type *qiuck.* At that point depending on your preference and your word processor, you can type over your error, erase the word and type it again, or press a key sequence that transposes the two incorrectly typed characters. Whichever method you use, your finished document bears no evidence of the original error.

Some changes are so minor that they can be

Tip 45:

Nasty Habits

Watch out that you don't let a program teach you bad habits that you carry over to other programs. Some word processors, for example, automatically save files for you, but others don't. Thus, you can wind up not saving a file in a different program and then losing your data.

Text Editing

fixed by transposing two letters (which can be done with a single keystroke in some word-processing programs); more major changes may entail typing over a word or erasing it and re-typing another. During this retyping process, the old word either disappears beneath the new one (this is called *overwrite* mode) or is pushed aside to make room for the new word (this is called *insert* mode). Overwrite and insert modes may go by different names in different programs, but if a word-processing program doesn't have both, it doesn't deserve the name. When you start an editing session, some programs assume you want to write over old words, and others assume that you want to insert them. Either assumption can be changed easily and is entirely under your control.

Nearly all word processors contain a command to delete a word to the right of the cursor (or the remainder of a word from the cursor to the next empty space on the right). A handful of word processors also allow you to delete a word to the left of the cursor.

Unlike a typewriter, a word processor does not require you to type a return at the end of a line. As you approach the right margin of the screen you simply continue to type. When you have typed more characters than will fit on the line, the program merely goes back to the last full word that will fit and begins a new line with the next word. That feature is called *word wrap*.

There probably are no word processors on the market today, at least for the IBM, that are not full-screen editors, that is, editors that will allow you to move the cursor around the screen at will and make whatever changes you have to make. How simple cursor movement is in a word processor is another matter. In some programs, moving to the beginning or end of the line requires you to type sequences such as CtrlQS or

CtrlQD (as in WordStar), while in others you may press a single key, such as Home or End (as in PCWrite) or Shift → and Shift ← (as in Volkswriter).

What happens when you have to make the same change many times? For example, suppose you have consistently misspelled *Cincinatti* and need to correct it to *Cincinnati*. To do that, you would use the word processor's search-and-replace capability. You must often be careful when using a replace. For example, in correcting *Cincinnati*, you may choose to specify that *inatt* should be replaced by *innat;* doing so would correct *Cincinatti*, but it would also make the word *inattentive* into *innatentive*. You must specify enough of what you are searching for to find only those instances that apply. You can, of course, search for a word or phrase without specifying that it be replaced.

A good word processor allows you to replace selectively, displaying each instance of the specified characters and letting you decide whether to replace it. An even better word processor allows you to use wild cards in the search. A *wild card* is a character that can be made to stand for any other character. For example, if you want to search for words that contain the letters *ing*, such as *single, things,* and *finger,* but you don't want the cursor to stop at every gerund in the document, you can use a wild-card search to find those words and skip all the ones ending with *ing*. Not many word-processing programs allow wild-card searches. One that does is PCWrite.

Block moves are electronically analogous to cutting and pasting. They allow you to mark the beginning and end of a piece of text to relocate it to any part of the document. One technique people use is to copy the block of text to three or four spots in the document, see where it works best, and then delete it in all but that place. The program should make marked text stand out somehow, either by using reverse video (dark characters against a light background) or by displaying the marked region in characters that are brighter or dimmer than unmarked regions. Some programs use both techniques: reverse video to indicate that you are still marking text and high intensity display to indicate the region that's been marked. Some programs, for unknown reasons, do not permit you to make multiple copies of a block of text. If you wish to move the same text into three or four places, you must mark it for each move.

You can also mark a piece of text and then write it to the disk as a separate file. If you do that and you give the new file a name that you have already given another file on that disk, you run the risk of irretrievably erasing the earlier file. A good program will not let you do that without warning. Some programs will tell you that the file exists and give you a choice of canceling the command, replacing the file, or appending the marked text to the end of the existing file.

Some programs are finicky about moving blocks of text around and limit the size of the block that you may move at any one time. Others set no limits. Some, Volkswriter Deluxe, for example, take a long time to move a block of text around. That tends to inhibit your making changes.

An inherent danger of moving text is that the commands you use to mark text for moving are usually the same as those you use to mark it for deleting. Recognizing that, a few programs do not irretrievably delete text. Rather, they set it aside in a portion of memory called a *buffer*, from which it can be recalled. Such an undelete feature is usually limited to the most recent deletion. Thus, if you accidentally delete a piece of text while you are moving it, and you then delete a single line intentionally, you can re-cover only the single line. Microsoft Word, PCWrite, MultiMate, and The FinalWord are among the word-processing programs that have undelete functions.

A clear advantage of the undelete feature is that it enables you to move text from one document to another without first creating an intermediate file. That's done by marking and deleting the block from the first file, thus putting it in the buffer. If you want to retain it in the first file, use the undelete command (the text will remain in the buffer even after it reappears in the document). Then switch to the second file, find the place where you want to insert the text in the buffer, and retrieve the deleted text from the buffer. Once the text is in the buffer, it remains there as long as you are using the program (unless the program has a limit on document size and needs the buffer space for the document you are editing). If your word processor has an undelete command and switches files easily, you can probably save a bit of disk space this way. Writing a lot of intermediate files clutters disk directories and makes for a lot of housecleaning time, because you must go back later to delete files that existed only to move text from one document to another. Ideally a word processor should allow you to move material between files without using either the undelete feature or intermediate files. WordPerfect is one package that has this capability.

Some word processors allow you to mark a piece of text, issue the search command, and then search for the marked text. By doing so you avoid the risk of making typing errors when the program asks what you are searching for and thus wasting time searching for something that does not exist in the document. You can also search for hidden characters that control how the document looks.

Tip 46:

Transpose and Undelete

A word processor that contains an undelete command also makes it possible to transpose entire words easily. All you have to do is delete one of the words, skip to the beginning or end of the other and issue the undelete command. In some programs using the undelete feature to transpose words puts just that deleted word in the buffer, erasing its previous contents. Other programs seem not to work that way—they let you delete a single word without clearing the contents of the undelete buffer.

Formatting Text

Decimal Alignment

Some programs use the ruler line to set decimal alignment for tabular material, enabling you to type $654.321, $1234.56, and $4567.890 on separate lines and watch them automatically line up correctly on the decimal point. No word-processing program for use in statistical typing should be without decimal alignment.

The formatting feature that can be used to classify all word processors is whether they let you see what your document looks like as you edit or permit you to see formats only when you print. The former are "what you see is what you get" word processors; the latter are called *character-oriented* word processors. Some character-oriented programs contain a command that allows you to preview the appearance of a printed document; however, you cannot edit the document in that mode, so if there's anything about it you don't like, you have to bounce back and forth from preview to edit modes until you get it right.

Virtually all word-processing programs contain a ruler line, which is used by the program to set left and right margins, tab stops, and paragraph indentation. In some programs, the ruler line appears on the screen when you start an editing session, but you can always turn it off. In some cases you can move the ruler line to any part of the screen you wish.

The ruler line can be changed easily and should be a part of the file you are using. That is, once you have set the ruler for a particular file, it should not change until you reset it. You don't want to have to reset the margins, tabs, paragraphs, and so forth every time you edit the file. Some programs allow you to save rulers as separate files and then move them around into other files. One nice feature is a ruler that allows you to set the left margin to the right of the paragraph indentation in order to produce hanging paragraphs.

Centering lines between the margins is another generally available feature of most word processors. Some programs allow you to mark a block of text and center all lines in the marked region, others permit you to center only a single line at a time.

When text is spaced so that every line ends the same distance from the right edge of the screen (or paper), it's said to be *justified*. Unjustified text is called *ragged right*. All word processors enable you to justify text or to leave it unjustified, as you wish.

Deleting words and sentences, inserting new ones, and moving and deleting paragraphs and sentences throughout the document are operations that produce a screen with some lines so long that they extend beyond the edge of the screen and others that are only a few words long. To reform paragraphs when such disarrangement happens, you can issue the wrap-paragraph or reformat command. No reasonable word-processing program lacks the capacity to wrap paragraphs (some do it automatically, not requiring you to issue a command). Paragraph wrap reforms the entire paragraph, moving words back and forth from line to line until all lines fit within the margins.

The problem with many wrapping features is that you always seem to be at the end of a paragraph when you want to wrap it, and you can wrap only between the cursor and the end of the paragraph. So, to make your work neat, you have to move the cursor to the beginning of the paragraph and then issue the command. Ideally, the program should be able to find the beginning of the paragraph itself, send the cursor there, and then wrap. WordPerfect is such a program. Unfortunately, that is one of the few programs with which we are familiar that can wrap an entire paragraph no matter where the cursor lies. However, if your program allows you to customize the keyboard (as PCWrite does) or if you own a program such as PROKEY, which allows you to use keyboard macros (see page 105), you can create a command to do so, as we'll show you later.

Printing the Text

More than any other software, word processing is sensitive to the kind of printer you use. Most programs will let you choose the print style from within the program and give you enough freedom to emphasize as little as one character within a single word, either by using boldface, double strike, or italic fonts. Chapter 3 looks at some of the printer–word-processing issues.

Most word processors are also fairly flexible concerning headers, which are lines of text that appear at the top of each page (such as the title of the document or a page number), and footers, which are at the bottom of the page; some of the older programs, however, only allow headers. A few programs allow you to have different headers and footers on right and left facing pages or multiple-line headers and footers, or both.

Automatic page numbering is a feature that cannot be missing if a program is to be called word processing. Slightly less crucial, but not much, is conditional paging, which lets the user define where a page can break, thus avoiding breaking in the middle of the table, diagram, or other element of the text that must remain intact. In any event, when material is inserted or deleted, page breaks and page numbers should be adjusted automatically by the program.

Your ability to control line spacing varies from program to program. It's usually easy to mix single and double spacing within the same document or even the same paragraph.

Printers, at their fastest, cannot begin to approach the speeds with which computers can transfer characters. For example, to make a copy of the file of the first draft of this chapter took around eight seconds. The chapter at that point was approximately 32,600 bytes long. It took around four minutes to print the chapter— roughly 35 times longer than it took to save it.

That's why it's important to be able to continue editing one document while printing another. Some programs allow you do that, and some don't.

With some word processors, the printer can be made to pause to allow you to enter text. Microsoft's Word, PCWrite, and The Final-Word have a pause for text entry, but Multi-Mate, WordStar, and Volkswriter do not.

Sometimes it is more efficient to edit smaller documents than to try to work on a single, long one. Chain-printing documents allows you to link one file to the end of another and tell the printer to print one after the other. You can then enter a single command and go off to do something else while the program consolidates the files and prints them as one document. Some programs, such as WordStar, require you to buy a separate program in order to chain-print files. Others, such as XyWrite and PCWrite, do not. Similarly, PCWrite permits you to "nest" files for printing. That is, you can insert a command in a PCWrite file that will cause the program to begin printing a second file before the first is completed and then to resume printing the first. (You can nest one file within another up to six deep—file A calls file B, which later calls C, which calls D. When D finishes printing, the program resumes printing C, then finishes B, and finally returns to and finishes A.

One of the more frustrating problems with printing a document is that if the printer jams for some reason, you usually have to begin printing again from the start of the document. Typically, when the jam has been cleared, you've lost less than a page of material, but the word-processing program requires you to print the whole document again. You may have to stop printing altogether and re-edit the document so that you can resume printing on the

Tip 48:

Chain-printing Boilerplate Paragraphs

The ability to chain-print and nest files can be invaluable if you deal with documents that often consist of variable boilerplate paragraphs.

page before the one where the jam occurred. Some programs allow you to stop the printer and then to resume printing on the previous page, the current page, or the next page.

Editing, formatting, and printing are the nuts and bolts of word-processing software. But what of the rest of the program? There are three other areas that users should weigh when they're deciding which word processor to adopt.

Ease of Use and Ease of Learning

WordStar is famous for being difficult for newcomers to learn and to use. Many of its advocates insist that that difficulty is repaid many times over when you consider the power of the program, but that's an arguable position. A number of programs are on the market today that, for most users, are more than sufficiently powerful and that are far easier to learn than WordStar. There are also a few word-processing programs that are as powerful as WordStar *and* easier to learn and use.

Tip 49:

Switching Word Processors

It's worth pointing out that once you've gotten the hang of one word-processing program, it's usually relatively easy to learn another. The commands, most of the time, behave in roughly the same ways. The cursor moves in response to the arrow keys, the Enter key starts a new line, and so on. Some programs even mimic the behavior of other programs so that if you forgetfully slip into using an older command it still works. PCWrite, for example, will do most of the same things that WordStar does. If you use WordStar commands such as Ctrl T, C, R, F, J, and so on you will get the same result as when you used them in WordStar.

One question that you should ask is how easy is it to get started? In one sense, that's easy to answer: does the software come with an "install" program? If so, that program has to be run first in order to run the word-processing program. That's not always easy. For example, with WordStar, if you have more than 340K, a bug in the WordStar Version 3.3 Install program becomes apparent. (The bug was reported and the solution supplied in Barbara Chertok's regular column in *PC Report*, the BCS IBM User Group newsletter. The solution she supplied was worked out by Bill Claff of The Boston Computer Society.) When you load the install program (the file called WINSTALL.COM on your WordStar disk), it tells you that you have too little memory. To fix the bug, you need the DEBUG program that comes with DOS.

A cautionary note on using DEBUG is in order here. The following suggestion involves patching a program. When you do that, you are fiddling around directly in the program's code. The kinds of mistakes you can make are simple enough—substituting 01 for 10, for example—and they can remain invisible for a long time. When they do surface, it may even seem that something else has gone awry. In short, be careful. Don't try patching a program unless you have made a back-up copy. If you can't make a copy of the program, don't patch it at all unless you are fearless, an expert, or—preferably—both.

Load DEBUG in drive A, load a copy of WINSTALL.COM in B, and type

DEBUG B:WINSTALL.COM

When the underline cursor appears, type

E 2D4

The "E" invokes the Enter command, and the sequence '2D4' is the address you are "entering." You will see the following display on the screen.

xxx:2D4 7C etc.

The "xxx" can be any number.

The next step is critical. You must change 7C (the hexadecimal equivalent of 115) to 72 (the hexadecimal equivalent of 104). To do that type

72<RETURN>

Do not enter a space, because in this part of the DEBUG program, the space bar will take you to the next address in the program. Press the Enter key.

The last step is to make the change a permanent part of the program by using the Write command of the DEBUG program. Type

W

The screen will display the message that you are writing some number of bytes. When the underline cursor reappears, type

Q

to quit the DEBUG program and return to the operating system. Now when you use the install program you will able to install WordStar on a machine with more than 340K.

Not all word-processing programs require an installation. Volkswriter and PCWrite, for example, boot immediately. PCWrite comes with a batch file called GO. Type the word "go" and you are told how to begin. No installation is necessary.

Help

It is inconceivable that a software developer would bring to market a word-processing program that doesn't contain some sort of help facility that the user can call to the screen in the midst of using the program. The question is whether the help text is easy to use, accurate, and extensive. "Easy to use" is a subjective judgment. Some people don't like pull-down menus of the sort that WordStar and Volkswriter use. A pull-down help menu is one that appears at the top of the screen and that looks like a screen that has been pulled down over the text. A portion of the text that was on the screen remains in view. In most cases, the display of a pull-down help menu is under your control. You can display it or not as you wish. Some users prefer a pop-up help facility, which fills the screen when the help command is given. Nothing is more frustrating, though, than a slow help text that fills the screen. It seems to take forever, and it discourages users from seeking help when they have small problems. A help text that fills the screen must be fast, easy to gain access to, and easy to discard.

One test of a help text is its accessibility. Some help texts permit you to move in one direction only. If you want to review something, you have to start at the beginning and walk through the text until you reach the part you want. If you then want to get somewhere else, you have to quit the help facility and begin again at the top. The alternative is the kind of help facility that allows you to "browse." Once you are in the help facility, a good program lets you wander at will until you have answered questions to your satisfaction.

Macros

The popularity of ProKey is testimony to the value users place on ease. ProKey, a program developed by RoseSoft, is a utility program that you can tell to "remember" a particular keystroke sequence so that you can execute that sequence later merely by pushing a key or two. The shorter sequence is called a *macro* (short for macroinstruction, a bit of computer jargon meaning an instruction to do a large job). Macros can make short work of tedious jobs. For example, an entire paragraph that must be repeated frequently can be assigned to a single macro, which can be invoked every time that paragraph is needed.

Some word-processing programs, such as PCWrite and Samna, contain a macro facility. PCWrite, for example, allows you to "collect" one macro from the keyboard. You don't have to name the macro, as it is executed by pressing the (unshifted) PrtSc/* key. Samna also allows you to collect macros from the keyboard.

Usually, you can build a macro in two ways: in immediate or deferred mode. In the immediate mode, you can collect the macro from the keyboard, meaning that you tell the program to begin remembering what you type, give the macro a name—such as Shift F1 or Alt Z—type the text or commands you want to reproduce or re-execute, and then tell the program to stop remembering. As you press each key, the command it represents is carried out immediately as well as remembered by the macro program or facility. Later, when you type the name you've given the macro, the program electronically reproduces the keystrokes you originally typed.

In the deferred mode, you give the macro a name, write out the sequence of commands or the text that you wish to reproduce (using a specific syntax that the program understands), and then store the macro for later use. When you are just beginning to use macros, it's best to stick with the immediate mode if it is available, because you can concentrate on executing the commands rather than learning the syntax the software developer has constructed.

One of the first macros to write if your word processor allows it, or if you buy a pro-

Tip 50:

Macros and RAM Disks

If you have a memory expansion board with a RAM disk on it, write the macro so that it saves the file to the RAM disk, which will be much faster than writing it to a floppy. If you do that, though, play it safe by writing a macro that won't allow you to leave your word-processing program until you've copied the file in the RAM disk to a floppy. That way you can't lose your work by quitting the word processor and turning off the machine.

gram like ProKey, is one that enables you to save files easily. Try to reduce the number of keystrokes it takes to save the file. In WordStar you have to type Ctrl K D. With ProKey, you can make it Ctrl F1. There's not much you can do to reduce the time it takes to save a file, but you can make it easier to get in the habit of saving files often.

Most of the time when you use a microcomputer you see only a small portion of the file. On a spreadsheet, for example, you can view only 20 or so rows of a sheet that's 250 to 8,000 rows deep. The screen is a window on a larger entity. Some programs allow you to split the screen, usually horizontally, into smaller segments and then to find other parts of a spreadsheet model. Windows, in a word-processing program, allow you to view different portions of the same document. Some word-processing programs take that one step further and enable you to split the screen in two and have more than one file on the screen simultaneously. That kind of capability marks a fairly sophisticated program. Right now few word processors allow it; The FinalWord, PCWrite, Microsoft Word, and Epsilon 1.22 are several that do.

Don't waste your time trying to use windows to do fine editing—that is, to move around and pick up many minor bits and pieces that you have to move here and there. Unlike a printed page, which can hold more than sixty lines, the screen shows you only 21 or 22 lines of text at a time. If you split a screen into two windows, you're down to 10 or 11 lines. That's fine for moving fairly large chunks of text that are easy to locate, but not convenient for more complex operations.

Windows

Tip 51:

Doing Windows

Windowing allows you to mark text in one window and to move it to the part of the document in the other window, even if the other document is a different file. That means that you can move text without creating an intermediate file.

File Management

The acid test for a well-designed piece of software is how it behaves if you try to save a file when the disk is full or the disk drive door is open.

WordStar allows you to cancel the command and to delete files from the disk. Unfortunately, if you do not have back-up copies of the files, you cannot delete them. What's more, WordStar won't let you list the sizes or dates of the files, and if you try to insert a new disk and perform the save, the system hangs and gives you a system error message telling you that there was an error in reading the drive or an error in reading a sector. They will be followed by the "Abort, Retry, Ignore?" prompt. Whenever that appears and you have been using WordStar, you are out of luck. You are at the operating system level and you cannot get back to the program.

Much more friendly is a word processor that allows you to insert a new disk. Some programs even allow you to quit without quitting. That is, you can leave the document, go into DOS, copy or delete files from the disk that's too full, type a single word that returns you to the exact spot in the document where you left off, and then save the document. The process is called opening a DOS shell, meaning in effect that you suspend the operation of the word-processing program and freeze, but not close the file on, the document. XYWrite and PCWrite allow you to use shells.

A number of word processors allow you to run some other programs from within them, but they are subject to some limits. If your word processor allows you to reenter DOS without closing the file, though, you should be able to run other programs. For example, you cannot run 1-2-3 from within WordStar. Thus, if you use WordStar and are in the midst of a report that requires you to update a 1-2-3 file, you must save your work, leave WordStar, load and run 1-2-3 file, update the file, save it, leave 1-2-3, load and run WordStar, open the file you were working on, find where you left off, and insert the updated 1-2-3 file.

With a word-processing program that allows you to open a DOS shell, you can freeze a document in memory, load and run 1-2-3, update the file, save it, leave 1-2-3, reenter the document exactly where you left, and insert the updated 1-2-3 file.

Some word processors, and other programs as well, require that you use no more than half the space available on a disk. The rest of the space is used for scratch files (which are analogous to scratch pads, in the old days of paper and pencil). That means that you are really paying $6 for every $3 disk you use with such a program.

Tip 52:

Renaming Active Files

Another test of a good word-processing program is whether it permits you to rename a file while you are working on it, save it under the new name, and continue working on it under the new name. That may sound like a bell or whistle you can do without, but it can make life easier if you need multiple versions of a document that differ in minor particulars or if you want to experiment with a document while keeping the original version intact. If you have ever globally replaced something and wished you had not, but could not get out of the file without losing more work than was comfortable, you will appreciate the ability to rename a file before saving it. By doing that you can at least recover some of the work. If you can only save a file with all the changes in place or quit without incorporating any changes, you cannot recover.

Much is often made of the performance (speed) differences between word-processing programs. Now and then a program comes along that is remarkably slow to respond to your commands, but problems of responsiveness are generally minor. There are, however, two areas in which performance often differs dramatically and which can affect your productivity using a word processor.

The first is the time that it takes to move a piece of text from one place to another in a document. Some programs can move text almost before you know it, whereas others work up an impressive sweat going back and forth to the disk as they huff along from where the text was to where you want to put it. Some, given a large enough piece of text, throw up their hands in despair and ask you to try a shorter piece. Those programs are better than cutting and pasting by hand, but not a lot.

The second area in which performance is important is the speed with which you can save and load files. It varies enormously, and it makes a difference, because the longer you must wait the less likely you are to save your files often. And anyone who has used a microcomputer for long carries the scars inflicted by lost files. The file that represented the original draft of this chapter, from the beginning to this point, took just over eight seconds to save in PCWrite. It was 37,292 bytes long at that time, approximately 30 double-spaced pages. That's a fast save compared to a number of other programs. In WordStar and Volkswriter, it took nearly a minute.

6/Advanced Word-processing Tips

Happy letter! Tell him—
Tell him the page I didn't write;
Tell him I only said the syntax,
And left the verb and pronoun out.

Emily Dickinson, *Part III, Love*

Reading a File from Another Word Processor

Because word processing software must support printers and because printer manufacturers have generally accepted the American Standard Code for Information Interchange (ASCII) for use with their machines, word-processing programs are limited to a relatively well-defined format in which they may store files. Consequently, in most cases, there is little to keep you from reading files created on a word processor different from yours. If you use, say, XyWrite and you want to send a document to someone who uses Perfect Writer, you should be able to send a file that can be read directly into the computer with no further ado. You might first have to remove any embedded formatting commands, but that is usually relatively easy. Software developers don't make much of this point, but the ease with which you can move files from one word processor to another makes it a snap to switch word-processing software. It also means that there is no particularly strong reason for adopting a single word-processing program as *the* standard for an entire organization.

Two widely used word-processing programs, WordStar and MultiMate, however, do not produce standard ASCII files. To get around that, you can "unWordStar" or "unMultiMate" files easily.

If you were to print a sentence with high ASCII characters using WordStar's print program, it would automatically convert the characters to a standard roman typeface. If you moved that sentence into another word processor and tried to print it, there is a chance that it might not print the unusual characters. It is more likely that it would print the characters as italic versions of the letters that were originally typed. Some programs can search for and replace those characters, but that's a tedious job in a long document.

One of the easiest ways to convert a WordStar file into a file that can be read by any other program is to run the WordStar file through Lotus' 1-2-3 first. (This technique was suggested by BCS member Dr. Steven Shapse and was reported in Barbara Lee Chertok's column in *PC Report,* the BCS IBM User Group newsletter.)

First, you must rename your WordStar file, because 1-2-3 recognizes files only if their names end with the extension .wks or .prn. In this case, the WordStar file must be given a file name ending with the extension .prn. That will make 1-2-3 treat it as it would a file created with its own /Print File command. Play it safe, however, and preserve the original version of the WordStar file by using the DOS COPY command rather than the REName command.

Enter the following command:

COPY WordStar_name WordStar_name.PRN

You'll wind up with two identical files, only one of which 1-2-3 recognizes.

Now load 1-2-3. When it is on the screen, type

/F

That puts you into the file management part of 1-2-3. Select the import option by typing

I

You'll then be presented with the choice of reading the file as text or numbers. Notice the line in the text choice that says "Enter each line of file as a single label." Each line in the WordStar file will be read into 1-2-3 as a single long label in column A. Type

T

The file will be read into 1-2-3. If the file appears not to read, and you get the error message

Part of file is missing

hit the Enter key. The error message should disappear and the file should appear on the screen. The message is usually caused by the file's lack of an end-of-file marker that 1-2-3 recognizes. When the file appears on the screen, it will look no different from any of the WordStar files with which you are accustomed to working.

Now, to make it ready to be read by another word-processing program, type

/PF

That is, enter the print command, but instead of sending the file to the printer, send it to a file on the disk. When the program prompts for a file name, it is probably best to save space on the disk by using the same name as you used when importing the file. The program will ask whether you want to cancel the command to print the file to disk or to replace the file you used earlier. Answer that you want to replace. Type

Filename.PRN

When the program asks for a range, remember that each line of the file was read as a single label, so you only have to specify the last row in column A that contains a line of the text file. When you quit 1-2-3, you will have a file on your disk that is in an ASCII format that can be read by any other word processor.

What if you don't own 1-2-3? A look at the table of ASCII characters shown in the appendix reveals that each of the characters that WordStar uses to mark the ends of words is in the so called high ASCII set. That is, they have been assigned decimal values of 129 or greater. Their values are also exactly 128 greater than the roman letter that they represent. Thus the "σ" (the Greek letter sigma) has an ASCII value of 228, and the letter "d" has a value of 100. If you make that substitution in the sentence above, the word "saiσ" becomes "said." If you were to try to print "saiσ" on an Epson FX80 or FX100 printer, you would get "sai*d*."

The following BASIC program reads a WordStar file character by character. If the ASCII value of a character is less than 128, the character is passed to a new file without any alteration. If the ASCII value is 128 or greater, the program subtracts 128 from the value and then passes the character to the new file. When it has read the last character in the WordStar file, the program closes the two files and displays the message "FINISHED."

```
10   INPUT "What is the name of the file
     to convert" ;I$
20   INPUT "What is the name of the new
     file" ;O$
30   OPEN "I", 1, I$
40   OPEN "O", 2, O$
50   A$=INPUT$(1,1)
60   IF ASC(A$)>=128 THEN A$ =CHR$
     (ASC(A$)-128)
70   PRINT #2, A$;
80   IF EOF(1)=0 THEN 50
90   CLOSE
100 PRINT "FINISHED"
```

This program is not limited to use with WordStar; it can be run with any program that uses the high ASCII set. (By the way, don't drop the semicolon in line 70 or you will wind up with a file in which each character is on its own line.)

Reading Spreadsheet and Data Base Files into a Word Processor

Spreadsheet and data base management system programs make relatively limited demands on a printer. There are just not that many different ways to print ten digits. If you wish to massage the headings and labels that you put in a spreadsheet file or data base report, or if you want to include in a word-processor document tabular materials that you produced in your spreadsheet or data base program, it is easier to move the file directly into your word-processing program than to retype all the columns or reports.

Reading a spreadsheet file into a word processing program is almost as easy as the manuals lead you to believe. The problem is that it's so easy that the manuals toss off the explanations as mere asides.

There are two steps in the process of moving a spreadsheet or data base file into a word-processing program: saving the file in the first place and reading the file into the word processor. Most people have most of their problems at the time they save the file. The following discussion centers on saving spreadsheet files. If you are interested primarily in database files, don't despair—the essential problem is the same.

The single most important mistake people make is to save a file in the normal manner and then try to load that file into the word processor. What they end up with, if they get anything at all, is a screen full of strange characters—little faces, mathematical symbols, arrows, Greek letters, hearts, spades, clubs, diamonds, and a sprinkling now and then of letters they recognize as labels or field names they typed into the spreadsheet or data base.

Files saved with normal commands (/File,Save in 1-2-3; /Store,Write in VisiCalc Advanced Version; /Save in SuperCalc) contain two kinds of information: how the screen looked when the file was saved and what has to be done to make it look that way again. The latter information concerns the formulas and logic of the spreadsheet model or the field length and relationships between fields in the data base. You need that to load your file again in the spreadsheet or data base program, but it only gets in

Tip 53:

Integrated Balance

Fans of integrated software will argue that it should never be necessary to use unrelated software packages. The reality is that if an integrated product has a good spreadsheet, its word processor or data base isn't equally good; if its data base is good, its word processor and spreadsheet tend to be weak.

the way of the information about how the screen looks. Unless you are trying to document the logical underpinnings of your spreadsheet models, all you need to do is reproduce the screen as it looked when you saved the file. That is, you want to perform what is called a formatted screen dump.

If you wanted to make a paper copy of the file, you would use the spreadsheet's printing commands to send the information to the printer. To send it into your word processor, you send that information to a file on the disk instead of to the printer. In general terms, no matter what spreadsheet you use, the first step in moving one of its files to any word processor is to create a printable file on a disk. To prepare a 1-2-3 file to be read into your word processor, then, you would use the /Print, File command. In VisiCalc Advanced Version the command is also /Print, File. In SuperCalc³, the command is /Output, Display.

To move the file into your word processor, you need not change its name. Simply use whatever command your word processor calls for when you want to edit a document or insert one into a file you are already editing. Before you risk blowing yourself out of the water, however, make a back-up copy of the document.

Before you actually bring a file from a spreadsheet into your word processor, you can prevent one annoying surprise. VisiCalc Advanced Version, 1-2-3, and other spreadsheets for the IBM PC are set up to accommodate 8½-by-11-inch paper. Consequently, the default line length in those programs is in the neighborhood of 70 characters. For example, 1-2-3 sets the line at 72 characters, the left margin at column 4, and the right margin at column 76. At 12 characters per inch, that gives a neat, 6-inch line with room for a 1½-inch margin on the left and a 1-inch margin on the right. If the portion of the spreadsheet model that you want to move into your word processor exceeds the default line length, then the print file you create will become a multipage document. To check whether you need to reset the line length, remember that your IBM screen is 80 characters wide. If you have to scroll any part of the spreadsheet off the screen when you save the print file, you will probably have to reset the margins.

Few word-processing programs restrict you to 80-character lines, so as a general rule you should probably always reset the margin of a spreadsheet before you bring it into a word processor. It will be much easier to break it apart and move it around once you've got it on the screen of the word processor than it is to restore it to its original appearance after the spreadsheet program defines pages.

Remember, too, that using compressed printing mode (17 characters per inch) you can fit 110 characters on an $8\frac{1}{2}$-inch sheet of paper and still have 1-inch right and left margins. If you are willing to live with mixing compressed and pica or elite type on the same page, you can use a fairly long line for the spreadsheet-originated portions of your documents.

Resetting the Default Line Length

To reset the default line length in 1-2-3, type

PRINT, FILE, filename, OPTIONS,
MARGINS, left, right

Once you've reached the "left" and "right" levels of the OPTIONS subcommand, you can enter numbers that will redefine the margins.

SuperCalc[3] sets the default to 132 characters. To reset it, use the following command, filling in the width that satisfies your goal:

/OUTPUT, DISK, range, SETUP, WIDTH

In VisiCalc Advanced Version, use

/PRINT, SETTINGS, WIDTH

Panel A of figure 6–1 shows a spreadsheet model in which each of the characters in rows 1 through 4 represents six characters on the screen. That makes a print file that would begin in A1 and end in AM4, for a total width of 240 characters. Using compressed type, a file that wide can be printed on a wide-carriage printer, but only if you reset the margins to 240 characters.

Panel B in this figure shows how the printed file would appear if you did not reset the margins. A typical spreadsheet program puts on each page as much of a row as the default line length will permit. It does not then wrap the remainder of the spreadsheet row to the next printed line, but rather begins the next row of the spreadsheet model. The text continues that way until it finishes a full page (defined as some number of lines adjustable from within the spreadsheet program) and then returns to the first row of the spreadsheet file and resumes printing that row as the first line of the second page. If the remainder of the first row of the spreadsheet file is still longer than the default line length, the program once again stops printing the first row and begins the second row. It continues as it did with the first page and will come back to begin a third with the remaining portion of the first row in the spreadsheet model. So it continues until all the rows in the file have been printed.

Panel C shows how the pages can be re-assembled in order to restore the file to the way it looked on the screen.

Souping Up WordStar

Like other programs originally written for smaller machines, WordStar consists of a root file (or loader) used to load the main part of the

PANEL A

```
||||||||||||||||||||||||||||||||||||||||||||||||||||||||||||
------------------------------------------------------
Now is the time for all good brown foxes t
o jump over the lazy red dogs.  In Antarc
tica there are three kinds of penguins.
12345678901234567890123456789012345673390xxxxxxxxxxx
```

PANEL B

```
----------
  page
   1
Now is the
o jump ove
tica there
1234567890
----------
  page
   2
time for a
r rhe lazy
 are three
1234567390
----------
  page
   3
ll good br
y red dogs
 kinds of
1234567890
----------
  page
   4
own foxes
o jump ove
tica there
1234567390
----------
  page
   5
t
c

xxxxxxxxxx
----------
```

PANEL C

```
----------   ----------   ----------   ----------   ----------
  page         page         page         page         page
   1            2            3            4            5
Now is the   time for a   ll good br   own foxes    t
o jump ove   r the lazy   red dogs.      In Antar   c
tica there    are three   kinds of     penguins.
1234567890   1234567890   1234567890   1234567890   xxxxxxxxxx
----------   ----------   ----------   ----------   ----------
```

Figure 6-1: Spreadsheet Model

Learning Piecemeal

Whenever I needed a new function or had a new idea, I would page through the help facility until I found something applying to the problem. Then I would read the related manual page. In this way, I only needed to read those parts of the manual that applied at the time. This method caused less confusion while I tried to learn.

program in RAM, an overlay file consisting of a number of modules that contain the various program functions, and another overlay file that contains the help text, error messages, and prompts that appear on the screen as you run the program.

As a result of that structure, WordStar spends a lot of time reading the disk to load functions, display help text, and otherwise manage itself. Reading the disk is a slow way to get information. Of course, if your machine has only 128K to work with, there's not much you can do except try to speed things up a bit by increasing the number of buffers you are running (see chapter 4). If you have one of the standard multifunction boards, such as the AST Six-Pak or the Quadram Quadboard II, you can set aside a portion of RAM, which the system will read as though it were another drive. The system will still have to read the "drive" but because everything on a RAM disk remains stationary instead of spinning as a floppy disk does, the reads are substantially faster.

You then must copy the program files to the emulated disk. Unfortunately, that's the rub with WordStar: it always looks for the program in drive A, and you must designate the RAM disk as drive C. If you simply copy Word-Star to drive C, the first time the program looks for the overlay file it will go to drive A, and you'll have defeated your purpose. You have to make WordStar use drive C at all times. To do that, you can "patch" the WordStar program using DEBUG.

With the DOS disk containing DEBUG in drive A and a copy of your WordStar disk in drive B, type

DEBUG B:WS.COM

When the underline cursor appears, type

F 2DC L1 3 (ENTER) W

A message will appear that says the DEBUG program is writing some number of bytes (usually more than 5,000). When the disk drive light goes off, type

Q

which quits the DEBUG program.

Now you can copy WordStar to drive C and run the program from there. Depending on how much RAM you allocated to the emulation drive, you can also store document and non-document files there, too.

Some books about WordStar tell you that you cannot print a double-spaced WordStar document on a dot matrix printer but that you can do so on a letter-quality printer. If you use WordStar's Ctrl O S command to set line spaces at 2, however, you can print a double-spaced WordStar document on a dot matrix printer.

The real problem arises when you have imported a single-spaced file into the program and try to edit and then print it. (The following discussion assumes that the file that is read into WordStar is single spaced and that it contains two line spaces between paragraphs, not a single line space and an indentation.) WordStar sometimes reads the end-of-line markers in other programs as "^N" (control N), which is the command to insert a new line in a file. Consequently, when the file is moved into WordStar, each line contains a "<" symbol in the right margin. That symbol means there's a hard return at the end of the line and you can neither double space nor wrap paragraphs unless you remove all those returns. Fortunately, that's not hard to do, because you can search for the "^N" markers and replace them with soft markers produced by holding down the Alt key and typing 141, releasing the Alt key, and then holding the Alt key again and typing 138.

Printing Double-spaced WordStar Documents

Let's go over that again. Load WordStar and call up a document file that is single spaced and that ends each line with a "<". Type

^Q A [Press Ctrl, Q, and A simultaneously.]

When the "FIND?" message appears, type

^N [Press Ctrl and N simultaneously.]

When the "REPLACE WITH?" message appears, hold down the Alt key and type 141, release the Alt key, and then hold it down again and type 138. You cannot hold down Alt and type both 141 and 138. If you do, the symbol "^]" will appear as the search argument. You must release the Alt key after typing 141 and hold it down again to type 138. It will appear that nothing has been entered in response to the "REPLACE WITH?" prompt. The cursor, however, will not remain stationary. When you type Alt 141, the cursor will jump to the beginning of the line, to the left of the "FIND?" message. When you type Alt 138, it will move down one line. The program is not only recording the characters you are typing, it is actually carrying out the instructions that they represent.

When you are prompted for options, type

GN

Line by line, the "<" symbols at the ends of the lines will disappear. When the search-and-replace action is over, you reach the most precarious moment with the file. Do not replace or add any material until you replace the hard paragraph markers. Type

^Q A

When the "FIND?" message appears, you want to search for the spaces previously occupied by two hard returns (^N ^N), so you press Alt and type 141, press Alt again and type 138, and repeat that whole sequence.

The "REPLACE WITH?" message should appear in a surprising spot, directly beneath the "FIND?" message instead of to its right, where it customarily appears. Now type

^N ^N [Press Ctrl and N
simultaneously and repeat.]

Between each paragraph two "<" symbols now appear, one atop the other. Now if you issue a Ctrl B command to wrap a paragraph, it will wrap only the paragraph, not the file from the position of the cursor to the end.

Wrapping a Paragraph from Any Position

All word-processing programs use some sort of character or character sequence to mark the start of a new paragraph. For example, in Volkswriter the character is Alt 20 (¶). In WordStar, it is the two-character sequence Alt 138 Alt 141 ("<"). If the program allows you to search backwards for that marker, you can simply write a macro that searches backwards from the cursor until the marker is found and then executes the paragraph-wrap command. That can be done fairly easily in WordStar (versions 3.3 and later). Type

^QF ^N ^N

Then type

B (

when you are prompted for an option. That takes you back to the beginning of the paragraph plus one space. Before you issue the wrap command, (Ctrl B), you have to move forward one space.

In PCWrite, Ctrl PgUp takes you to the beginning of a paragraph, so the search is already performed for you. So if you add

%356=388,321

to your PCWrite ruler file, Ctrl F7 will wrap a paragraph from any place within the paragraph except the first line (where you would use F7).

7/Spreadsheets

As yet a child, nor yet a fool to fame,
I lisp'd in numbers, for the numbers came.

Alexander Pope,
Epistle to Dr. Arbuthnot. Prologue to the Satires

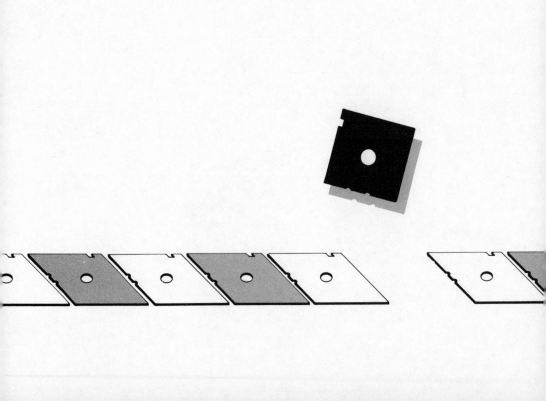

Even if you have never used an electronic spreadsheet or one of its paper forerunners, you have probably used the concept. If you've ever drawn a line or two from the top to the bottom of an ordinary, lined sheet of paper, you have created a spreadsheet. When you drew those lines, you created columns on a sheet that already had rows. It doesn't matter whether you filled those columns with household budget figures, the names of people to invite to a party, or the election results by precinct in your town.

Although they have been used to generate form letters and to plan the layout of a garden, spreadsheets are primarily number-crunchers. A spreadsheet can be used for most problems, mundane or esoteric, that involve manipulating numbers.

Whether it is paper or electronic, the spreadsheet is no more than a blank sheet (or screen, if you prefer) that has been organized into horizontal rows and vertical columns. The rows are numbered from top to bottom, just as they are on the paper spreadsheets that were once so widely used in businesses. The difference is that paper spreadsheets are usually only 40 rows deep, and electronic ones range from 254 to 8,192 rows deep. Paper spreadsheets are so narrow that they rarely, if ever, are sold with column identifiers analogous to the row numbers. Electronic spreadsheets, however, may be divided into almost 700 columns, so the columns are identified with letters from A through ZZ.

The intersection of a row and a column on an electronic spreadsheet is called a *cell* (some people also call it a *box*). As with paper spreadsheets, you can type numbers or letters in cells. If you type only letters, they are called *label* (or *text*) *entries*.

The first cell on the worksheet, which is what some spreadsheet programs call the file, is in the upper left corner of the sheet, at A1 (column A, row 1). To the right of A1 is B1, and below it is A2. In 1-2-3, the last cell, at the lower right corner of the sheet, is IV2048. Multiplan, a popular spreadsheet produced by Microsoft, numbers both rows and columns. The Multiplan equivalent of A1 is R1C1 (for Row1Column1), and the equivalent of B2 is R2C2.

On the surface there's not much difference between paper and electronic spreadsheets. Both have rows and columns and allow you to write letters and numbers in them. The electronic spreadsheet is bigger, but that's of no concern to people who've managed for years by doing their calculations on the backs of stray envelopes. So what's the big deal? Well, if you are one of the back-of-the-envelope people, there is no big deal, and you can probably ignore spreadsheet software for the rest of your life. However, if you keep running out of envelope back just when things get interesting or important, you're probably a latent spreadsheet user.

In a fundamental way, putting numbers on paper differs from putting them on a spreadsheet. Paper is an inert two-dimensional medium. When you write something on a paper you transfer the results of your thought. The electronic spreadsheet is an active, three-dimensional medium. When you "write" something on an electronic spreadsheet, you transfer the substance of your thought, and the spreadsheet displays the result. When you put something on a spreadsheet's screen, the spreadsheet does two things with it: it records what is on the screen and it records where it is located, the address of the element you put into the spreadsheet. Appearance is distinguished from position. What and where are separable. On paper, only the contents of an entry can be recorded, and you have to remember where you put the numbers.

Precisely because it separates information

about the number and its address, the spreadsheet allows you to refer to and manipulate addresses without regard to what those addresses contain. That is, in one cell you can say, "Take address A and subtract it from [or add it to or multiply or divide it by] address B." If address A contains a 6 and address B contains a 10, the cell in which you put the subtraction statement will contain a 4. As soon as you change A or B, the answer will change, but the addresses will remain the same.

Let's be more concrete. To add two numbers in A1 and B1, you first select a cell in which you will write the formula—say, C1; then you type +A1+B1 and a carriage return. As soon as you type the return you get an answer. If you change the number at A1, you get a new answer at C1. If you go to D1 and type +C1*B1 (an asterisk represents the multiplication sign in a spreadsheet) and a return, you'll get another answer. Now, by changing the numbers in A1 or B1, you'll see the changes ripple across the row of numbers. (The plus sign is required to tell the program that the characters you are typing are to be read as a formula and not a label. Because either kind of information is acceptable, most spreadsheet programs assume that you want to type a label if the first character you enter in a cell is a letter. To tell the program that the *A* in *A1* is the beginning of a formula, you have to alert the program by feeding it a character that has something to do with numbers. Alternatively, (A1+B1) is also acceptable as a formula.)

On a paper spreadsheet, if you discover that you have written a number incorrectly, you must change it and every other number that uses the first for some sort of calculation. On an electronic spreadsheet, the only number you have to change is the one you "wrote" incorrectly. The program automatically uses the new

Tip 55:

The Macro Miracle

I work primarily with Lotus' 1-2-3, and the greatest unexpected asset I found was using macros. Macros have changed my life.

value in all calculations that refer to the address in which you made the change.

There are hundreds of spreadsheets on the market today, although 1-2-3 is the most widely used. Because of 1-2-3's popularity with users, most of this chapter will be spent discussing some of the things that will make life with 1-2-3 a bit easier.

What Makes It Good?

Most people seem to build their models on a spreadsheet by starting in the first row and continuing down, rather than across the sheet. That practice indicates that the number of rows is an important consideration. Currently 1-2-3 has the lead in this respect; it has 2,096 rows. VisiCalc, VisiCalc Advanced Version, Super-Calc[3] and Multiplan have only about 254 rows.

You will probably never use all those rows, at least not on a machine that is restricted to 640K of memory. It is far more likely that you will run out of memory long before you fill all the cells in a worksheet.

Several other questions help determine how good a spreadsheet is. First, how long does it take to save a file? Saving your work often is a prerequisite to happy computing. Voltage spikes, power surges, and brownouts aren't very common, but they seem to come at the worst possible times. A PC will protect itself from hardware damage due to a power surge, but the cost of that protection is the erasure of any data in memory. Low voltages can also cause data to be erased. If you save your work ten minutes before the power goes off, you lose ten minutes of work. If it's just before quitting time and you haven't saved all day, you may as well have stayed in bed. The time it takes a program to save a file can encourage you to save your work or discourage you from doing so.

Second, how widely used is the program?

Although it has taken a shellacking in the marketplace lately, VisiCalc still has a strong user base, though it is not as widely used as 1-2-3. Multiplan, SuperCalc³, and SuperCalc² complete the big four of spreadsheets. Popularity is not necessarily a sign of superior programming, but it is important if you need support, since you're more likely to encounter someone who's using the same program and who may have solved exactly the problem that's bedeviling you.

Third, how easy is it to use? Some spreadsheets are easier to use than others, but all of the currently available spreadsheet programs are relatively easy to learn and to use. Super-Calc³ suffers substantially in comparisons with 1-2-3, Multiplan, and VisiCalc Advanced Version, all of which use full-word prompts while SuperCalc³ still uses single-letter prompts. If you come to Multiplan from another spreadsheet, it may take you a while to get used to Multiplan's alphabetic row/column designations. 1-2-3's help facility is very good, though it can occasionally be confusing for the newcomer. VisiCalc Advanced Version's help text is also good, though very different from 1-2-3's. Both are thorough and context-sensitive, and both allow the user to browse around in the help facility.

Finally, can you name a cell or range of cells? If the spreadsheet has a naming capability, as 1-2-3 and Multiplan have, you can give a cell a name, such as Adjusted Gross Income, or Net Operating Profit. You can also refer to names in formulas. That would allow you to type something like +Sales−Costs in a cell. The cell that contained that formula could be Btprofit (Bt for "before tax"), which in turn could be part of a cell with the formula +Taxrate * Btprofit. Naming cells differs from using labels to identify them. Labels are text strings.

Tip 56:

Naming Ranges in 1-2-3

1-2-3's ability to name ranges is a powerful capability, but it is sometimes quirky. If, in macros, your ranges begin acting unexpectedly, don't try to figure out whether you or the program is at fault. You'll save time by using range-name delete and starting over.

If you use a label in a formula, most spreadsheets will treat it as 0. (Thus, if you try to divide by a label, you'll get an error.) A name is a value entry that looks like a text string.

Besides the obvious advantage of having a number of often-used functions, such as @SUM, @MIN, @MAX, and @LOOKUP, built into a program, what makes a spreadsheet useful?

Replicating (Copying)

Often, the problem is not a matter of working out what a formula ought to be but of writing out the results of repeated applications of that formula. Working up a mortgage amortization schedule, for example, is really simple mathematics, and hand-held calculators often have PMT keys for the one figure that involves more than just elementary arithmetic. The only problem is that amortization schedules consist of the same calculations over and over for 240 to 360 lines.

If you use an electronic spreadsheet, all you have to do is work out the first line or two of formulas and then tell the program to copy those formulas into the next 23 or 28 lines. It does so and automatically adjusts the formulas to reflect their new addresses and changing basic data. Thereafter, all you have to do is supply a new interest rate or loan amount, and the program produces a new schedule in seconds.

Built-in Functions: The Use of "@"

Many of the standard formulas for performing calculations have been defined by the authors of spreadsheets and made into built-in functions. For example, if you wish to add a column of figures, you do not have to type "+A1+A2+A3+A4+A5+A6+A7+A8." The spreadsheet contains a "sum" feature called "@SUM" that allows you to type the following: "@SUM(A1 .. A8)." (Most spreadsheets follow the conventions laid down in the original version of VisiCalc and precede all built-in functions with the "@" symbol).

The mathematical formula for calculating a payment on a loan is

$$\text{Loan}*(\text{interest}/(1-(1+\text{interest})^\wedge-\text{time}))$$

It is not necessary to remember the formula for calculating the payment to amortize a loan. All you need to do is remember to use the "@PMT" function. Among the other formulas built into a good spreadsheet are those for calculating present and future values, net present value, internal rate of return, periods (for calculating the number of payments to amortize a loan), and rate (for calculating a rate given two sums and a period of time).

Any spreadsheet worth paying attention to also contains many other functions, including functions that find the largest or smallest value in a series, select a value from a table, round calculations to the desired precision, perform a variety of logical comparisons, and perform date arithmetic.

One of 1-2-3's surprising shortcomings is its collection of built-in financial functions. Although it does contain functions to calculate present and future values, internal rate of return, and net present value, it lacks functions to calculate a rate given a series of equal payments and to calculate the number of payments needed to amortize a loan. Another omission is that the functions for determining present and future value cannot deal with single sums but assume a series of equal values. The discussions that follow tell you how to get around all these limitations.

First, you should know how to use the figures in this chapter. All the worksheets illus-

Tip 57:

Saving Templates

Once you have written all the formulas that are involved in solving a problem, whether it is a mortgage amortization schedule, a trial-balance sheet, or a production schedule, you can not only save the specific information for that client but also use the sheet as the basis of a template for all other clients. They're easy to adapt.

Using Spreadsheet Financial Functions

trating the problems dealt with in this chapter contain the numbers we have entered and, beside them, the formulas used to produce the numbers. Whenever you see a formula in a figure, type it on your sheet in the place where the value appears in the figure. There's no sleight-of-hand here; the figure is not the way your screen should look.

All financial functions manipulate four values: the principal amount (*prn*), the term (*n*), the rate (*i*), and the payment (*pmt*). Given any three of those values, a financial function calculates the fourth. Present and future values (*pv* and *fv*) are simply names given to special solutions for the principal amount.

Let's begin with the simplest problem to solve. The "@PV" and the "@FV" functions of 1-2-3 calculate the values of annuities but not of single payments.

The general formula for the future-value calculation of a single payment is

$$FV = (1+i)^{\wedge}n$$

The general formula for the present-value calculation of a single payment is

$$PV = (1+i)^{\wedge}-n$$

As you can see, the only difference between the two formulas is the sign of the number of payments. If *n* is a positive number, you are calculating a future value. If *n* is a negative number, you are calculating a present value. Given either a present or future value, you can derive the other simply by dividing one by the amount given.

Calculating an Unknown Rate

The underlying mathematics of finding a rate, given only the term, the principal, and the payment, are complex and involve repeatedly approximating an answer. It's almost a form of controlled trial and error. Rather than guessing randomly, however, each time an approximation of the rate is calculated, the first guess is tested to see how close it came to producing one of the known terms. It's then adjusted to reflect the degree by which it missed the mark and is cycled through the same set of calculations again.

The key, of course, is making a good first guess. If the rate you're looking for is 13.75 percent and you start with 5 percent, you must make more tests to get close to the right rate. This solution uses the payment as the test measurement, so the starting guess is pulled from the relationship between the payment and the principal.

In the days before microcomputers and calculators, you calculated a payment by looking up a number in a table of financial values and multiplying the principal amount by that number. Here that number is called the *payment proportion*. In other words,

$$\text{payment proportion} * \text{principal} = \text{payment}$$

Given the payment and the principal amount, you can derive the payment proportion by dividing the payment by the principal amount. That is, the equation above becomes

$$\text{payment proportion} = \text{payment/principal}$$

When you deal with a series of equal payments, the payment proportion approximates but does not equal the actual rate used to calculate the payment in the first place. It's derived by taking a term equal to 1 plus the rate and raising it to the power of the number of payments. That is:

$$\text{payment proportion} = (1+r)^{\wedge}n$$

Because you're trying to isolate the rate, you have to take the root of both sides of that equation. Once you've done so, the equation becomes

$$\text{payment proportion}^{\wedge}(1/n) = 1 + r$$

Thus, the following is true

$$1 - \text{payment proportion}^{\wedge}(1/n) = r$$

Because the payment proportion is the same as the payment divided by the principal, the equation is

$$1 - (\text{payment/principal})^{\wedge}(1/n) = r$$

That equation gives a good starting guess. Once that is calculated, it is fed into a calculation of an approximate payment, and the result is compared to the actual payment. That is, the actual is divided by the approximation. The result of that calculation yields the degree by which the first approximation overstated the rate (actually the reciprocal of the overstatement). Multiplying the first approximation by the last calculation yields a new, lower approximation, which is fed into the same sequence of calculations.

Figure 7-1 shows the worksheet on which the set of calculations is performed. Only columns A and B are on the final sheet. To reproduce the sheet, you should type in column B the formulas shown next to the values. The figure shows the formulas that work for 1-2-3. If you use another spreadsheet, you may have to edit the expressions somewhat. If your spreadsheet doesn't contain "@PMT," "@PV," or "@ROUND" functions, use the alternative formulas shown in the figure.

If you do use the alternative formulas, be especially careful of parentheses. If you go wrong anywhere, it is probably because you made an error entering a parenthesis. You should also watch the "@INT" formula that is used to round the rate in B15. If you inadvertently use the 4 in B14, your sheet will show 0 at B15 and ERRORs at B16 and B17. The 10,000

```
           A          B          Formulas in column B
 1
 2
 3  prn1              65000
 4  term                360
 5  pmt              757.32
 6  test1          0.012291     1-(B5/B3)^(1/B4)
 7  approx pmt1    808.8983     @PMT($B$3,B6,$B$4)
                                   or +B6/(1-(1/(1+B6)^$B$4))*$B$3
 8  act vs approx  0.936236     +$B$5/B7
 9  test2          0.011507     +B6*B8
10  approx pmt2    760.3656     @PMT($B$3,B9,$B$4)
                                   or +B9/(1-(1/(1+B9)^$B$4))*$B$3
11  act vs approx  0.995994     +$B$5/B10
12  test3          0.011461     +B9*B11
13  approx pmt3    757.5270     @PMT($B$3,B12,$B$4)
                                   or +B12/(1-(1/(1+B12)^$B$4))*$B$3
14  round               4       4              10000
15  rate            0.1375      @ROUND(B12*12,B14)
                                   or  @INT(B12*12*B14)/B14
16  prn2          64999.72      @PV($B$5,B15/12,$B$4)
                                   or  (1-(1/(1+B12)^$B$4))/B12*B13
17  accurate to    0.999995     +B16/B3
18
```

Figure 7-1: Worksheet for calculating an unknown rate. Note that the third approximation, at B12, still does not produce the exact payment shown in B5. Because the rate shown in B15 is rounded, however, this model yields the correct rate, 13.75 percent.

shown on the sheet will round the calculation to four decimal places (as many decimal places as there are zeroes—you would use 100 to round to two places and 1,000 to round to three).

The model shown in figure 7–2 assumes that three test rates are enough to yield a correct rate. When the numbers involved are large and the rates are not very low (3 to 4 percent would be considered very low), three tests are usually sufficient. When the numbers are low, however, you may have to fiddle with the model. That's particularly true if the terms are short. Short-term loans—say, for 60 or fewer periods—require more approximations before they

will solve. In those cases, rather than extending
the sheet, you can take TEST3 and plug it in
where TEST1 is and run through the sequence
again as many times as necessary. If your
spreadsheet does not have a macro facility, you
can simply go to cell B6 and change the formula
there to +B12. That creates a circular reference
(*circular reference* is a term that describes a formula that either directly or indirectly uses itself
to calculate itself). If your spreadsheet contains
conditional macros, you can write a macro that
will, when invoked, run until the level of accuracy you desire has been reached. Such a macro
is shown in figure 7-3.

	A		B	
3	prn		18000	18000
4	term		60	60
5	pmt		400	400
6	test1		0.061473	0.009975
7	approx pmt	1	1138.272	400.1302
8	act vs	approx	0.351409	0.999674
9	test2		0.021602	0.009972
10	approx pmt	2	538.1075	400.0948
11	act vs	approx	0.743345	0.999762
12	test3		0.016058	0.009969
13	approx pmt	3	469.6052	400.0690
14	round by		4	4
15	approx		0.1927	0.1196
16	prn2		15331.93	17998.36
17	accurate to		0.851773	0.999909

Figure 7-2: Spreadsheet for
Calculating an Unknown
Rate

```
                              '{goto}b6~
                              '1-(B5/B3)^(1/B4)~
                              '   +b12~
name this cell RETEST         '{calc}~
                              '/xib17<0.9999~/xgretest~
```

Figure 7-3: A macro that retests for accuracy

Debugging Spreadsheet Formulas

When you have a formula that is giving you a problem, it's sometimes helpful to take it apart, piece by piece, and see how each smaller piece works. For example, imagine formulas such as

@DATE((B7 − 1900) + @INT((C7 − 1)/ 12),@MOD(C7 − 1,12) + 1,@DAY(D4)) + D5

Or

(P33*P36 − P34*P35)/(@SQRT (P33*P37 − P34^2)*@SQRT (P33*P38 − P35^2))

Developing those expressions is no mean feat, and debugging them can be exasperating. The second formula, which is used to calculate the coefficient of correlation, originally contained a dozen more parentheses than it does now. Such expressions are much easier to debug if you can deal with the "@INT," "@MOD," "@DAY," and "@SQRT" portions of them separately. Once each smaller piece is working satisfactorily, it can be combined with other pieces and you can gradually build a formula that works correctly.

To break the statement down into working parts, you should make three or four identical copies of the statement elsewhere on the worksheet and then edit them into smaller chunks. The problem in 1-2-3 is that to make three or four identical copies of the statement you must first go in and change all the value references to absolute references. In the "@DATE" formula that's not a big problem, but in the coefficient-of-correlation formula it's bothersome, especially since there is an easier way.

The easy way is to turn the entire expression into a label. When you copy a label from one part of the sheet to another, nothing changes, so you can make as many copies as you want without having to change any of the cell references. Turning an expression into a label in

Tip 58:

Helpful Macros in 1-2-3

Turning labels into expressions and vice versa are both candidates for quick macros, of course. The macro to turn an expression into a label would be

{edit}{home}'˜

The macro to turn a label into an expression would be

{edit}{home}{del}˜

Tip 59:

Naming Cells in 1-2-3 Macros

Watch out if you move, insert, or delete rows or columns. 1-2-3 doesn't adjust macros, and if you have specifically identified cells by their location (C15, for example), the macro will still go to that cell to execute whatever instruction it contains. For that reason, it is sometimes best to name cells and then specify the name in the macro. Should you then relocate the named cells, the macro will still be able to find the right place to carry out an instruction.

Tip 60:

Heavy-duty Slowdown

If your 1-2-3 macros on heavy-duty spreadsheets are taking longer than you want them to, maybe it's time to move on to a stand alone program.

1-2-3 is a matter of typing:

F2Home'

That inserts an apostrophe (the single quotation mark) at the beginning of the expression. When you press Return, the program will read the expression as a label. You can then copy it to any part of the sheet and none of the cell references will change. To turn the label back into an expression, press F2, Home, and then Del. That removes the apostrophe and allows the program to evaluate the expression as an expression again.

When you try this technique, you will notice that any values that depend on the expression that you turn into a label will change. Like all spreadsheets, 1-2-3 evaluates labels as 0. When you turn the label back into an expression, the other expressions will read that expression as you intended. Think about that for a moment. If you can turn expressions on and off simply by adding an apostrophe, then it is just as easy to write a macro that will conditionally turn off expressions depending on the outcome of other expressions.

For example, suppose you have constructed a worksheet to analyze the results of a test-market mailing, and at one point in the analysis you must select the highest of *A, B,* or *C.* Each is produced by using a slightly different formula, and the result of the formula must be fed into further calculations that also use slightly different formulas. (If you aren't familiar with analyses, in which using different formulas to deal with the same data is common, think of taxes. The presence or absence of certain kinds of income or expenses can trigger the need to use different tax calculations as well as different tax tables.) One approach is to select the appropriate result and then erase the others from the worksheet. However, if you must keep feeding in the data from a variety of tests and if you have erased formulas, you must keep reloading the original model.

Thus, you need to write a conditional macro like the one shown in figure 7–4. It is predicated on the use of four possible results and the selection of the largest.

```
/XIB16<A17~{GOTO}C16~{EDIT}{HOME}'~{GOTO}D16~{EDIT}{HOME}'~
/XIB17<A17~{GOTO}C17~{EDIT}{HOME}'~{GOTO}D17~{EDIT}{HOME}'~
/XIB18<A17~{GOTO}C18~{EDIT}{HOME}'~{GOTO}D18~{EDIT}{HOME}'~
{GOTO}F6~((B8*B12)+(B9*B13)+(B10*B14)+(B11*B15))*E6~
```

Figure 7-4: A Conditional Macro

Although macros make life easier, after you've gained some proficiency with them, you find that you are creating fairly complex sequences that are really close to being programs in their own right. You'll develop a library of routines that you can adapt for use with a large number of models. That means that you will have to begin editing your macros.

Because 1-2-3 has such a rudimentary editor and because its macros are only labels, you can sometimes save a lot of time and effort by writing and editing your macros in your word processor and importing them to 1-2-3.

The advantage of doing this is that you can do such things as mark a piece of the text that you have to repeat frequently, such as "{right}", and then copy it as often as needed rather than typing it again and again. What's more, you can easily develop your own short-hand and use your word processor's search-and-replace function to flesh out the document with 1-2-3 syntax before you import the file to 1-2-3.

For example, rather than typing "{del}-{del}{del}", you could type "{d{d{d", and rather than "{right}" or "{left}", you could use

Debugging Macros

">>" or "<<". The thing you must watch out for is using a shorthand sequence that might also be used as part of a command or as an operator (that's why "<<" and "{d}" were chosen; "<" could be part of a logical comparison, and "d" could be part of "/WDR", and you wouldn't want to wind up with something like "A1{left}B1" or "/W{del}R", which the program would not process. A bit of planning and reference to the manual can get you over that hurdle, though.

If your word processor supports it (Volkswriter and PCWrite do), go to the end of the word-processing file, press Alt and type 26 (using the numeric keypad). That will be recognized as an end-of-file marker by 1-2-3, and the macros will import cleanly. If you are using WordStar, type Alt 154, which will show on the screen as ^Z. (That's a single character, not the two characters "^" and "Z", so don't try using Shift 6 and Z to produce it.) If you can't add Alt 26 or Alt 154 to the file, 1-2-3 will read it but will give you a "PART OF FILE MISSING" message. The only part that is not there is the end-of-file marker, so you have nothing to worry about. Just type a Return and the macros will appear on the screen.

You can also edit macros more easily in a word processor than in 1-2-3. To edit macros, you must write the ranges containing the macro or macros to a file using /PF and then read the file into your word processor. Edit it and then send it back. There is a limitation, however, to the size of the macro you can move into your word processor. If the macro is more than about 75 characters wide, it will not fit on the 1-2-3 screen, you will not be able to put the entire macro in a .prn file. If your word processor will read a 1-2-3 worksheet file (one with an extension of .wks), and few can, you can send the entire file to the word-processing program and

Tip 61:

1-2-3 Macros from a Word Processor

If you use your word processor to generate the original file of macros, don't forget to give it the file-name extension .prn, or 1-2-3 won't recognize it as an "importable" file.

then strip out the macro.

In VisiCalc Advanced Version, storing and creating macros, which are called *keystroke memory sequences,* is entirely different from storing and saving them in 1-2-3. However, you can still write and edit them in a word processor and move them into the program. To see how you do it, start with a simple worksheet file and collect a macro from the keyboard. Save the file using the old /Storage, Save (not the new /Storage Write) command. The old file format is an ASCII text file. The macro you collect will appear near the beginning of the file immediately following the formatting definitions, beginning with the sequence "/K=x" (where "x" is the single-letter name of the macro). The characters that follow are commands that the macro carries out. A VisiCalc macro to delete three columns, for example, would appear in the file as the sequence. "/K=A/D3CY", and one to go to cell H67 would be "/K=B>H67^R".

Once you've edited the macros, save your word-processor file as you normally would and then reload it in VisiCalc with /Storage,Load. Don't forget to use the .vc extension, though, or VisiCalc won't recognize the file.

Techniques of Spreadsheet Design

Some problems are easy to define but so tedious to work through on paper that people often settle for less complete or less sophisticated analyses than they know are possible. Because the spreadsheet not only does the necessary calculations but also feeds intermediate results into further calculations, it lets users easily do what used to be considered "advanced" analysis. Analyzing a lease-or-buy decision is an excellent example of the power of a spreadsheet. This will not be a large model, but it will incorporate many important elements of a large one, so it is worth taking some time to go through step by step.

In general terms, the following model analyzes the lease-or-buy decision in the light of the effects of the investment tax credit (ITC), Accelerated Cost Recovery System (ACRS) depreciation, the cost of capital, the cost of borrowing money, the tax bracket of the company buying the property, and the present values of all those elements.

The model shown below assumes that you are using a spreadsheet of sufficiently recent vintage to contain some built-in financial and logical functions. This model uses "@PV", "@IF", and "@PMT."

Questions about the actual financial implications with which the model deals will not be covered here, except insofar as they dictate certain uses of the spreadsheet's functions. When you set up a relatively large spreadsheet model, it's best to organize it according to what you are doing in various places on the spreadsheet. Most models should have at least two major divisions.

The first section is the input area (see figure 7-5). This is the "what-if" section of a spreadsheet model. There should be nothing in the input area of the sheet except hard numbers that represent your assumptions.

The second section of the sheet is an output area. This is where the number crunching takes place. The output area should consist entirely of the formulas that give you your answers. Spreadsheets allow you to protect cells selectively to prevent their accidental erasure by inexperienced users. Keeping all the formulas together makes it easier to lock them up and thus prevent such accidents.

If you have to look up values in tables (depreciation schedules, tax tables, price lists, rate and tariff schedules, and so on), you should put a table area on the sheet. Most tables will contain only hard numbers. Occasionally, however, a table may be calculated from values entered in the input area of a model.

Finally, if you are going to use the results of the analysis in a report, you should have a report area to which you send those numbers that will be incorporated into a report. That makes it easy to move them as a block into a word processor. This model has no report section.

Not all models need all elements, but many large models often do. In programs like 1-2-3 and VisiCalc Advanced Version, the sheet is recalculated according to the logic of the model (the so-called natural order of recalculation), so it doesn't much matter where those sections of the model are. In a spreadsheet that is recalculated by row or column only, it's best to put the input area above and to the left of the output area and the report area beneath and to the right of the output area. If you must later add rows or columns to the model, you can do so without breaking up other parts of the sheet.

Panel A

input	input		input				
input	input		input		table	table	table
input	input		input		table	table	table
output	output		output		table	table	table
output	output		output				
output	output		output				

Panel B

input	input	input						
input	input	input						
input	input	input						
			output	output	output			
			output	output	output			
			output	output	output			
						table	table	table
						table	table	table
						table	table	table

Figure 7-5: Spreadsheet for Analyzing a Lease-or-buy Decision

The table area can be anywhere if your tables are made up of hard numbers. When you are calculating tables, their location on the sheet may affect how often you have to perform a recalculation before you get a correct answer.

In panel A in figure 7-5, the table area is damaged by the addition of several rows in the input area, and the input area has to be reorganized after a column is added to the output area. Adding rows or columns to sections of the model shown in panel B leaves the other sections of the model intact.

To Buy or Not To Buy

To help clarify this discussion, several spreadsheets will be presented here. It is assumed that you are seated at your micro, actually entering the figures and formulas that are printed here.

For neatness' sake, we've set formats so that dollar amounts show a dollar sign, a comma, no decimal places, and parentheses for negative numbers. Percentages are formatted to show the percent sign and two decimal places.

The input area of the sheet starts at A1 and goes to D11. All the numbers in A1 through D11 are typed in as shown in figure 7-6. Enter them on your spreadsheet.

```
       A            B            C          D
 1 input area
 2
 3 life of lease or loan                    10
 4 cost                           $200,000
 5 borrowing                      $200,000
 6 lease payment                   $37,500
 7 annual maint                     $4,500
 8 loan interest                    15.00%
 9 investment tax credit             8.00%
10 tax rate                         30.00%
11 cost of capital                  15.00%
```

Figure 7-6: Input Area of a Spreadsheet for Analyzing a Lease-or-buy Decision

Notice that in this figure the investment tax credit is 8 percent, not 10 percent. If you take the full credit (either 10 percent or 6 percent), you have to reduce your depreciable basis by half the amount of the credit. As an alternative, if you take the entire cost as your depreciable basis, you have to reduce the credit by two points. The model is set up to deal with the effect of either alternative.

Figures 7–7, 7–8, and 7–9 show the output area of the sheet, which starts at A15 and goes to D45. The first formula on the sheet is at D15 and calculates the amount of the investment tax credit (ITC) using the value of the property in D4 and the ITC rate shown in cell D9. The formula at D16 calculates the depreciable basis of the property depending on whether you elected to use the full credit and reduce your basis or reduce your credit and depreciate the full cost of the property. It uses the "@IF" and the "OR" functions of a spreadsheet. The next formula, at D17, uses the spreadsheet's payment function to calculate how much the annual payment is. The calculation at D18 gives a discount rate for the purposes of calculating present values. In this kind of problem, the after-tax cost of borrowing money is the rate to use. Finally, D19 contains a calculation that is used to tell a later formula where to find depreciation rates in the table section of the sheet.

```
12  A             B           C       D       D        E        F
13  output area
14
15  investment tax credit       $16,000  +D9*D4
16  depreciable basis          $200,000  @IF(@MIN(D9=0.1,D9=0.4),D5-(D15/2),D5)
17  payment on purch            $39,850  @PMT(D5,D8,D3)
18  discount rate               10.50%(1-D10)*D8
19  table offset                     3  @VLOOKUP(D3,A50..B52,1)
20
```

Figure 7-7: First Part of Output Area of a Spreadsheet
for Analyzing a Lease-or-buy Decision

21	A	B	C	D	E
22		ord	p.v.	ord	p.v.
23	periods	interest	interest	depr	depr
24	1	$30,000	$27,149	$18,000	$16,290
25	2	$28,522	$23,359	$38,000	$31,121
26	3	$26,823	$19,880	$32,000	$23,717
27	4	$24,869	$16,681	$28,000	$18,781
28	5	$22,622	$13,732	$24,000	$14,568
29	6	$20,038	$11,007	$20,000	$10,986
30	7	$17,066	$8,484	$16,000	$7,954
31	8	$13,648	$6,140	$12,000	$5,399
32	9	$9,718	$3,956	$8,000	$3,257
33	10	$5,198	$1,915	$4,000	$1,474
34	11	$0	$0	$0	$0
35	12	$0	$0	$0	$0
36	13	$0	$0	$0	$0
37	14	$0	$0	$0	$0
38	15	$0	$0	$0	$0

Figure 7-8: Second Part of Output Area of a
Spreadsheet for Analyzing a Lease-or-buy Decision

39	A	B	C	D	D
40	pv of depr costs a.t.			$133,547	@SUM(E24..E38)
41	pv of interest a.t.			$132,304	@SUM(C24..C38)
42	pv of lease pmts a.t.			$225,554	@PV(D6,D18,D3)
43	pv of lease pmts p.t.			$188,204	@PV(D6,D8,D3)
44	p.v. maint costs a.t.			$15,809	@PV(D7*(1-D10),D11,D3)
45	leasing advantage (buy)			($484)	+D4-D15+D10*(D42-D40-D41)-D43+D44

Figure 7-9: Third Part of Output Area of a Spreadsheet
for Analyzing a Lease-or-buy Decision

Type the formulas in column D exactly as they are shown in the second column D of the figure. If you have entered the same values as are shown in figure 7–6, you should get the values that are shown in figure 7–7. If there's a difference, keep in mind that dollar amounts have been formatted to show no decimal places. If you have not formatted the cell at all, for example, the payment at D17 will show 39850.41250 in a twelve-character column.

The portion of the output area shown in figure 7–8 is where the real advantage of using a spreadsheet becomes apparent. Doing this part of the analysis on a hand-held calculator is a matter of repeatedly entering the same formulas, jotting down results, and then entering still more formulas to massage the first set of results. With a spreadsheet, all you have to do is develop the first set of formulas and copy them down the sheet. If this had been a month-by-month schedule, columns B and C would have stretched down the sheet for another 110 rows.

The four formulas on which this part of the output area is based are

B24   @MAX(@PV($D$17, $D$8, ($D$3–A23))*($D$8), 0)

C24   +B24*((1+$D$18)^−A24)

D24   @IF(A24>$D$3,0,@VLOOKUP(A24,$C$50..$F$65,$D$19)*$D$16)

E24   +D24*(1+$D$18)^−$A24

The first of these formulas gives the interest payable in any year (or month if the numbers in column A are months). It uses the "@PV" function of the spreadsheet, because the unpaid balance on a loan, the basis for calculating the interest due, is in fact the present value of the remaining payments discounted at the rate the lender is charging. Because the number of periods shown in Column A can continue beyond the term of the loan, the "@PV" function is enclosed within a "@MAX" to prevent the calculation of negative interest charges.

(If you are not using 1-2-3, ignore the "$" symbols that appear in these formulas. Those symbols tell 1-2-3 that a cell reference is absolute—that is, it is not to be changed when copies of the formula are made. In VisiCalc and other spreadsheets, the cell references that contain the dollar signs would require a "No Change" response during replication.)

The formula at C24 calculates the present

value of the interest for the period. The formula at D24 checks first to see whether the periods number in column A is greater than the depreciable life of the property. If it is, no depreciation is calculated. If not, the depreciation for the period is fetched from the table at C50..F65. This is where the table offset in D19 comes into play. The depreciation table in C50..F65 (shown in figure 7–10) is set up so that it can be used with 3-, 5-, and 10-year properties and can be expanded to cover 15-year properties. The small table labeled "offset table" in A50..B52 is used to convert the life of the property into an offset number so that you can automatically tell the program which column to look in when it has to find the right depreciation figures. Without that smaller table, every time you wanted to look at properties with different depreciable lives you'd have to edit the expression at D24 and copy it into the cells below.

	A	B	C	D	E	F
46	A	B	C	D	E	F
47	table area					
48						
49		offset table		yr	ACRS lookup tables	
50	3	1	1	0.29	0.18	0.09
51	5	2	2	0.47	0.33	0.19
52	10	3	3	0.24	0.25	0.16
53			4		0.16	0.14
54			5		0.08	0.12
55			6			0.1
56			7			0.08
57			8			0.06
58			9			0.04
59			10			0.02
60			11			
61			12			
62			13			
63			14			
64			15			
65						

Figure 7-10: Depreciation Table

The formula at E24 is a copy of the one at C24, and gives the present value of the depreciation by period.

Once you have those four formulas on the sheet in row 24, copy them into the cells below (rows 25 through 38).

The last section of the output area is where the advantage or disadvantage of leasing the property is calculated (see figure 7–9). All the raw figures are on the sheet at this point, and all that remains is to put them together. The first two formulas, at D40 and D41, add up the total of the present values of the depreciation and interest calculations. The next three—D42, D43, and D44—use the "@PV" function again to calculate the present values of the lease payments before and after taxes and of the after-tax maintenance costs.

The last formula in the output area tells you whether to lease or buy the property. If the result of the calculation is a positive number it is more advantageous to lease. If you get a negative number, the property should be bought (assuming you trust your assumptions). The formula says: the leasing advantage equals the purchase price minus the ITC plus tax rate times (pv of lease pmts a.t. minus pv of depr costs a.t. minus p.v. interest a.t.) minus p.v. of lease pmts p.t. plus p.v. maint costs a.t. That formula is translated into cell references in D45. If the answer is positive, the property is a candidate for purchase. If it is negative, it should be leased.

Using Booleans

One of the things that people often do, almost without thinking, is to make conditional decisions—they test the water and choose one of two competing alternatives. Spreadsheets allow people to mimic that behavior by using the so-called Boolean functions.

The first step to mastering a spreadsheet's Boolean features is familiarity with Boolean operators. The four basic arithmetic operators—the plus sign ("+"), the minus sign ("−"), the asterisk ("*") for multiplication, and the slash ("/") for division—enable values to be combined in some way. Boolean operators enable values to be compared. When you use Booleans you deal with three basic operators: greater than (">"), less than ("<"), and equal to ("="). Those three elements can be combined to yield three more: greater than or equal to (">="), less than or equal to ("<="), and not equal to ("<>").

Logical Comparisons Using IF

The principal Boolean function in any spreadsheet is the IF statement. IF statements are not difficult to understand. In fact, they are frequently used in commonplace situations: "if it is raining, I'll carry an umbrella; otherwise I won't." In more formal terms, the IF statement is constructed as follows: IF *X* is true, then do *A,* else do *B.* The key sequence to remember is IF. . .THEN. . .ELSE.

In an IF statement, Boolean operators test whether some condition is true. So the entry in an actual spreadsheet might look like this:

@IF(A1>B1,C1,D1)

That expression tests whether it is true that A1 is greater than B1 and returns C1 if it is and D1 if it is not. As shown in figure 7–11, the IF statement can be represented as a branch.

Figure 7–12 adds another branch by illustrating the following expression:

@IF(condition, CASE ONE,(@IF(condition, CASE TWO, CASE THREE)))

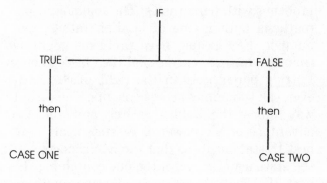

Figure 7-11: IF Statement Structure

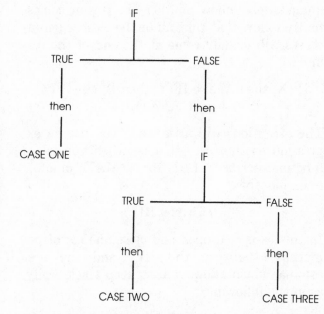

Figure 7-12: More Complex IF Statement Structure

Nesting IF Statements

Many of the problems that have to be solved in the real world are complex, and the answer to one question is just another question. In those cases, the spreadsheet is still useful. All you have to do is modify the IF statement a bit, and it can still help you choose between competing alternatives. The typical approach is to "nest" one IF statement within another. Most attempts to nest IF statements fail because of problems with parentheses. The commonest parenthesis fault is one of location rather than number. Few people have problems counting from one to three or four and then back to one. Putting parentheses in the right places, however, can sometimes give people fits. The easiest way to beat the problem entirely and still take advantage of the power of IF statements is to nest IF statements so that the ELSE portion of the statement is always the one containing the next IF. That means never allowing an IF to immediately follow another IF. If you consistently follow that rule, all of the closing parentheses will usually come at the end of the formula.

IF(X, then A, else IF(Y, then B, else IF(Z, then C, else D)))

The exceptions will arise when you use an expression as the test—that is, when you use a function such as "@MIN" or "@MAX" or a formula like this:

0.6*(A1+B1).

In this case, you open and close one set of parentheses between the "IF" and the first comma, which allows you to keep track easily, as in the following:

@IF (@MAX(P. . .Q), then A, else @IF (@MIN(G. . .F), then C, else D)

AND and OR

Often, the test that an IF statement must make is more complex than a simple TRUE-FALSE statement will allow. What do you do, for example, if your choice is between two alternatives but three or four tests are necessary before you can make the choice? For instance, in an investment decision, you would want to measure a series of things before you chose to buy. If any one of the things in the series failed to meet all your investment criteria, you would not buy. In Boolean terms, if any one condition is false then all are treated as false. The AND statement is used to express this concept. Alternatively, there are times when if any one condition is true, then all are treated as true. The OR statement represents this situation. VisiCalc, Multiplan, and SuperCalc³ contain AND and OR functions.

Imagine, for example, that you want to test for three conditions, A1>=B1, A1>C1, and D1<E1. In a program with an "@AND" function, the statement would read:

@AND(A1>=B1,A1>C1,D1<E1)

(SuperCalc doesn't use the "@" symbol, but the rest of the statement would be the same.)

Tip 62:

Alternative Uses of "@SUM" and "@MIN"

In 1-2-3, for some reason, Lotus has chosen to use an unusual form of AND, OR, and NOT. Rather than using the conventional "@NOT (list)" form of the function, you must insert "#AND#" or "#OR#" between each comparison in the list. If you have several arguments to test, the result is an expression that, as shown below, is difficult to read.

@IF(B1<C1#AND#D1=D3#AND#B1>A1
  #AND#A1<C2,@SUM(A1..A10), C5*C6−3)

  or

@IF(B1<C1#OR#D1=D3#OR#B1>A1#
  OR#A1<C2,@SUM(A1..A10), C5*C6−3)

If your problem is best solved by an AND or an OR statement, you can get the same result in 1-2-3 using the "@SUM" and "@MIN" functions. 1-2-3, like SuperCalc and Multiplan, gives a value of 1 to a true statement and a value of 0 to a false one. (VisiCalc displays the words TRUE and FALSE on the screen.) In logical terms, that can lead to an absurdity such as $3 + \text{TRUE} = 4$, but it allows you to use "@MIN" to substitute for "#AND#" in 1-2-3. If any of the required conditions were false, the program would give FALSE or 0. Since 1-2-3 uses 1 and 0 to represent true and false and since the program allows you to use logical operators within many functions, "@MIN(B1<C1,D1=D3,B1>A1,A1<C2)" will produce 0 if any one of the tests is false. Only if all are true will the statement produce a 1. Thus, you can use "@MIN", with its easier-to-read list of arguments, within an IF statement any time you might use "#AND#". The following IF statements, for example, give the same results as the ones above that used "#AND#" and "#OR#".

@IF(@MIN(B1<C1,D1=D3,B1>A1, A1<C2),B5,C5)

and

#NOT#@MIN(B1<C1,D1=D3,B1>A1)

The "@SUM" function also permits you to use logical operators. The 1-2-3 program reads only 0 as false; it will interpret any other number as true.

8/Data Bases and DBMS Software

Now go, write it before them in a table, and note it in a book, that it may be for the time to come for ever and ever.

Isaiah, 30:8

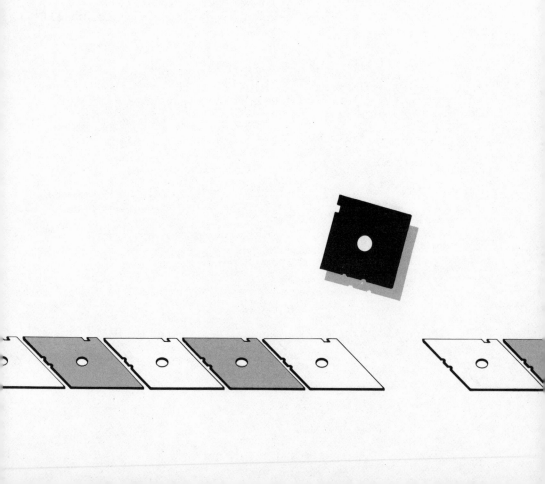

When you use data bases and data base software you approach the underlying logical structure of the software more closely than you do when using any other kind of application software. As a consequence, it is safe to say that most data base programs are really high-level languages. In some newer versions of older data base software, such as dBASE III, the successor to dBASE II, or in altogether new data base software, such as Cornerstone, a layer has been added to the program to make it easier for novices to use. The layer may enable new users to set up simple data bases quite easily. Beneath those layers, however, the programs remain essentially the same. Their structures are similar and the essential concepts are unchanged; experienced users can still use these programs to solve complex information-management problems.

This chapter is not for the experienced data base programmer. It is aimed at those who are looking for an introduction to data base concepts beyond that found in any data base manual. Although the text covers generic data base theory and procedures, the tips will often zero in on specific software packages. dBASE II and III, as the present data base leaders, receive extra attention as 1-2-3 and WordStar did in earlier chapters, but because the total number of users for data base programs is smaller than that for spreadsheets and word processors, and because the terminology varies so much between packages, the product-specific information will not be included in the general text.

A data base is a collection of information about a single topic. Programs that enable you to extract, add, delete, and change information in the collection are data base management systems (DBMS). Whenever the term *data base* is used in this chapter, it refers to the data itself. DBMS will refer only to the programs.

Tip 63:

dBASE's User Base

Don't minimize the importance of dBASE's user network and add-on products.

Tip 64:

dBASE Clones

The dBASE II clones are coming. They will be cheaper and will have fewer bugs, but will they be any more successful than all the IBM PC clones?

Tip 65:

Programming a Data Base

Decide early in your planning exactly what you want to do. Create all the logical subsets of your files at the start. Although the structure of most data bases is relatively easy to change, you'll have a lot more trouble changing the programs (or procedures or command files) that you've written.

One of the obstacles to understanding DBMS is the jargon used to describe them. Things that are simple are often wrapped in terminology that makes them appear complex. Confusion is compounded by lack of agreement over which terms to use. The same thing may be called a *field,* a *data item,* a *data element,* an *elementary item,* or a *relation.* To paraphrase Mark Twain's comment about New England weather, DBMS jargon has a sumptuous variety. Using so many words to identify the same thing is unnecessary and only serves to make DBMS programs seem hard to understand and to use. If you use DBMS programs that use terms other than those used here, don't despair. It may take a bit of effort to make the connections, but the underlying entities and concepts that the terms describe are the same.

Files, Records, and Fields

One of the words you see frequently in computer books and magazines is *file.* Files can be a number of things—a program, a collection of data, or a collection of other files—but all files share one characteristic: they are units of storage. No matter how large or small it is, the entity saved is defined as a file. Since storing information is essential to our idea of a computer, the concept of the file is essential.

It is important for you to understand that this chapter does not describe how information is stored on a disk. There is a significant difference between the physical and logical organization of storing information, and this chapter will describe only the logical organization.

A file is sometimes said to be analogous to a file folder, but that's an oversimplification. A file folder can be merely a disorganized receptacle, a place where you store information that you haven't the discipline to throw away. The files you manipulate with a computer are much more coherently structured. Each consists of *records* that contain all the information relevant to a single subject. If your address book were the file, for example, each of the names, addresses, and telephone numbers it contains would be a record (see figure 8–1).

Each record in a file is made up of *fields*. To continue the address-book example, your friends' names are fields within their records, as are their street addresses, cities, states, and zip codes.

Fields contain *values*. A value, in this context, should not be thought of in the same way it is in a spreadsheet. By the time information gets to the CPU, everything has been translated into binary code and can be represented as a series of 1s and 0s. Thus, the numerical value of the name *Janson* differs from the numerical value of the name *Jansen*. When you look at those words you use optical character readers to distinguish between them, but the machine has to use the numerical difference between the ASCII values of *e* (ASCII 101, binary 1100101) and *o* (ASCII 111, binary 1101111).

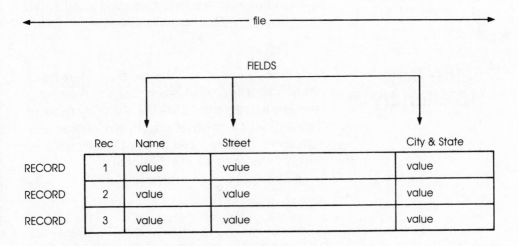

Figure 8-1: Structure of an Address-book Data Base

Tip 66:

The ASCII Bridge

Don't think everything
must be done within the
data base. It's only a tool.
Other popular programs
may do specific things
better. Use 1-2-3 for what-
ifs; use FORTRAN or
APL for number-crunch-
ing. Having a smooth
ASCII bridge between
your data base and other
products is essential.

A data base is analogous to a nest of boxes,
with files containing records, which in turn contain fields, which contain values. After values,
you begin to deal with bytes and bits.

Word processors and spreadsheets also use
files, records, and fields. Your spreadsheet budget, when you save it, becomes a file. Each of
the cells in the spreadsheet is a record. Some
records contain labels, some contain numbers,
and some formulas. Part of each record is a field
that tells the program what kind of record it is,
and other parts of the record are fields defining
the row and column of the spreadsheet where
the record is located, the size of the record, the
value of the record (if it is a formula or number), the characters in the record if it is a label,
and so on.

In a file created with a word processor, records and fields are much less highly structured,
a reflection of the fact that a word processor
does far less with the data you feed it than do
spreadsheets and DBMS programs.

When you use a DBMS, you deal explicitly
with files, records, and fields. Consequently, you
must be more familiar with the basic operations
of information processing than you need to be
when dealing with a spreadsheet.

The Data Dictionary

Somehow you must tell the program what fields
you will be using, what those fields will contain,
how large they are, and the other attributes
that will distinguish the information in your
data base. In short, you define the elements of
your data base in a data dictionary.

For example, the expression

field	width	type
first:name	20	char

is the definition in a data dictionary of a field
called FIRST NAME. (Some DBMS pro-

grams—dBASE II and III, for example—do not permit spaces to be used in a field name when the data dictionary is set up. To produce a field name like FIRST NAME, a colon is used to represent the space. When you extract information from your data base, however, the colon is suppressed and a space appears.) Like a lexical dictionary, a data dictionary consists of definitions, although in this case the details do not concern pronunciation and so forth, but the name by which the field is known, its size, and the data type, which restrict the kind of information you can enter in that field.

Defining the field size is something that can be intuitively understood. The only thing that should be said about it is that you should try to allow enough space to clearly identify the information that you will store in the field. Don't, for example, allow only eight spaces for a last name or ten spaces for a company name or street address. On the other hand, if you can expand coded information when you prepare reports, you can keep field sizes relatively small—one or two spaces—and add more fields. Most DBMS programs place interdependent limits on the number of fields and characters that a record may contain, and you have to work within those limits. If you are allowed 1,500 characters for a record and 20 fields, you cannot have 19 ten-character fields and one 1,320–character field.

Data types are what they sound like. DBMS software generally insists that you define how the data you enter will be treated by specifying whether the field will contain characters, numbers, dates, currency, or calculations. (Not all DBMSs accept all those data types.) Some things, such as zip codes, are often thought of as numbers but rarely used that way. To a DBMS, a zip code is just a string of characters. You will never add, subtract, or multiply one zip code and another, so define them as characters. Remember, they are still distinguishable as values and if you have to put things in order by zip code, the table of ASCII values that is used will give you the correct ranking of zip codes in ascending sequence from the lowest to the highest.

Numbers that you will manipulate arithmetically should be defined as numbers. Similarly, you should define dates as numbers. Ideally, a DBMS not only should correctly format dates but also should allow you to perform some basic manipulations, such as being able to say something like, "Give me all records for the date of March 1, 1986, and thirty days thereafter." Unfortunately, you'll rarely be able to put the question in terms that are that much like ordinary English—at least not yet.

It is at this stage—that of creating the data dictionary—that you often must make major decisions. Among them are the ways that fields affect one another. You may also have to decide whether data must be entered in a field or whether a default value can be accepted. Some DBMS software allows you to establish such defaults when you set up the dictionary. When you use defaults, if no entry is made in a field, the program will supply a preset value that was established at the time the dictionary was set up.

Some DBMS software also requires you to define any access limitations at the time you set up the data dictionary. That is, you may wish to prevent other users from reading, using, or deleting information in a field or file. If the data base requires the protection that limiting access implies, it should also contain provisions for an audit trail. Whenever you grant access to a user, you open up the possibility that data can be changed. An audit trail allows you to record the changes made in the data base.

Some fields in a record may have to be defined as keys at the time a dictionary is estab-

Tip 67:

Plan Ahead

Don't interpret that apparent ease as meaning that you don't have to think about the nature of your information requirements. More than any other kind of software, a DBMS program requires you to think through your objectives carefully *before* you take to the computer. Spreadsheets and word processors are like blank sheets of paper. The DBMS is a kind of black box. Something may be in there, but unless you know what you are looking for and how to tell the program that, you might easily overlook things.

lished. Keys will be discussed in more detail later, but in general, they are fields used to identify records. A record's primary key uniquely identifies that record.

To create your data dictionary, the program you are using will probably use a command such as DEFINE, as in dBASE II and III, or CREATE, as in R:Base 4000.

Many DBMS programs make the creation of a data dictionary quite easy. Some, for example, prompt you for the field names, field sizes, data types, and other information, by asking you to position the fields on a screen. When you want to put information into the database, the same screen appears as a data entry form.

Data Entry

One of the reasons for computerizing a filing system, which is the function of a DBMS program, is to allow you to organize and reorganize information to suit a wide variety of purposes. The first step, though, is to enter the information in the files; thus, one of the first things to ask is "How easy is it to create or edit a form for entering information in the data base?"

There ought to be two ways to enter data in any data base. The first is to enter it via some sort of form that you create using the editor function of the DBMS. Some DBMS programs contain primitive line editors; others give you a full-screen editor that operates like a limited word processor. A DBMS as popular as dBASE II will usually promote the development of a variety of form-generation programs that can be used with the DBMS to make the creation of an entry form simple. Using such forms is a matter of entering records one at a time.

You can also enter records in batches. That is, using a word processor, you enter data in a file; it is accumulated there one item at a time but items are not transferred to the data base individually. When enough records have been

Tip 68:

Only What's Needed

If information is worth
keeping in a data base,
then it's worth trying to
retrieve. Otherwise you'd
throw it out, right?

Tip 69:

KnowledgeMan's Syntax

KnowledgeMan was writ-
ten by eggheads for egg-
heads. IBM's SQL syntax
is both an albatross and
an advantage, depending
on the user's background.

entered, all of them can be read into the data
base at one time. Most DBMS programs allow
you to read data from files created on your word
processor. The data will have to be in a format
that the DBMS can read and it will have to be
organized to match the definitions established
when you created the data dictionary.

The implication of a DBMS's ability to
read word-processor files is that it is relatively
easy to move data from one DBMS program to
another. The specifics of how to do that are beyond the scope of this book, but as long as one
program will read an ASCII file and the other
will produce one, you can move data from one
DBMS to another. The first step is to produce
the data you want to move and then to read it
into your word processor. If necessary, at that
stage you can add any delimiters that are required by the second DBMS, you can expand
fields, and so forth.

DBMS programs must be relatively intoler-
ant of data entry errors. It isn't reasonable, for
example, to expect that you would be permitted
to enter a name where the program expects a
telephone number. Nor should a DBMS accept
20159508 as a telephone number (the number is
two characters short of being valid). Such errors
are prevented by the validation techniques that
a DBMS uses. You have to tell the DBMS,
however, what the limits of validity are. For example, you may tell the DBMS that the value
in a telephone number field must be ten characters long and that no record can be entered in
the data base unless the telephone field is filled.
Few things are more difficult for the DBMS to
work with than randomly incomplete records.

Data Retrieval

More than data entry, data retrieval should
occupy your attention. Defining the questions
you want to answer and the information you

need for decision-making, customer service, or whatever other use you have for a DBMS, will go a long way toward resolving your data entry issues.

When you want to get information out of a data base you use the query language that the DBMS supports. Each DBMS uses a query language that is unique, but generally all fall into two main camps, those that use an SQL (structured query language) and those that use a QBE (query by example) language. Almost all the DBMS software available for the PC uses some kind of SQL.

In a DBMS that uses a variant of SQL, you might see a statement like this:

LOCATE FOR Name='LEV'

This is a sentence of sorts in the query language of dBASE II. LOCATE is the verb. In some DBMS programs the word to locate a record is SELECT. The FOR introduces a clause that specifies what you want located.

QBE languages take a fill-in-the-blank approach. If the address-book format mentioned earlier were used to find the name "LEV" in a QBE DBMS, the screen might look something like figure 8–2.

Tip 70:

R:Base Pluses and Minuses

R:Base 4000 needs its advanced report writer to be really functional for a large application. It is easier to use and often faster than dBASE II, but it's less powerful.

Name	Street	City & State
LEV		

Figure 8-2: Finding the Name "LEV" in a QBE DBMS

When you ask for the data base file into which you had entered the names, the blank form would appear on the screen. When you enter the string LEV in the Name field, the program would respond by filling in the remaining fields.

When you want to locate many records, do

Tip 71:

Program When Necessary

Maintain interactive procedures until you need to store a program, for example, because of a repetitive procedure. Don't clutter your data base with unnecessary programs. K.I.S.S.—Keep It Short and Simple.

the most stringent select first. If you want to contact all the New York customers who have bought something from you in the last six months and whose original purchases resulted from a mailing to an American Express (AE) card list, select FOR State='NY' (not Zip >09 . . .), then FOR Source='AE', then FOR their last purchase date. A select for last purchase date or source first would involve many extraneous records.

The way a computer can go through a list of 600 or 1,000 names and pick out all the ones that fit certain criteria seems magical. Of course, you know that you could do it yourself, but you would finish bleary-eyed, and in the time it would take you, the computer could have done it another 47 times.

The process isn't magic; it's the data-access method. For one thing, you wouldn't read every character in the file, and neither does the program. You'd read only the part of the record that you knew would permit you to accept or reject the entire record. That's what the program does. To use a different analogy, if the records were in book form, you wouldn't read every page just to find the three pages on which the topic you are interested in is mentioned. Neither does the computer. Both you and the computer would go to the index first to find the data that points to the appropriate record or records.

The index, if you tell the DBMS to use one, is kept in primary key order and points directly to the sectors and tracks on the disk where records are stored. That's another way of saying that the index file of a data base is a direct line from the logic of the file to the physical location of part of the data base. For the most part, if an index exists for a data base it is the responsibility of the DBMS to use it whenever you try to retrieve data. dBASE II requires you to specify that you wish to use a data base's index when you issue the USE command. Thereafter you generally don't have to refer to it.

A DBMS uses index files to speed the search for data. The files can make it appear that the entire data base is sorted by a field that you have defined as a key. In fact, no sorting has been necessary. If searches go slowly, multiple index files can speed them up considerably. Gradually, as data bases grow, the search slows down. At that time you create an index to the indexes in the data base.

One form of indexing that is used widely in DBMS software is the so-called B-tree. A B-tree is a multilevel index. Imagine that you want to find a particular key field in a record—a name, for example. If the data base contains 20 names, finding one won't take long, even if the search requires reading every record in sequence. If there are 500 names in the list, however, it will take much longer. A B-tree search, however, begins by comparing the value being searched for to the value in the middle position in the list. If the value of the entry in the middle of the list is greater than the value of the item being searched for, the search goes to the position halfway between the middle and the beginning of the list. The first two comparisons, then, eliminate three quarters of the items in the list.

In order to go through a list of 20 values, you need only ask four (yes/no) questions to narrow the list down to one value. If there are 1,048,575 values in the list, it will take 20 questions. To explain it differently, if your tree has 20 levels, it can accommodate 1,048,575 values, half of which will be on the 20th level.

Figure 8–3 illustrates how a B-tree works when the data base has 20 names.

Alsop	Moberg
Bernoff	Moulter
Brout	Pitlor
Byrne	Preston
Donner	Rosen
Frankston	Sessions
Hodgman	Solodar
Kahl	Tarter
Law	Underkoffler
Lawrence	Weissman

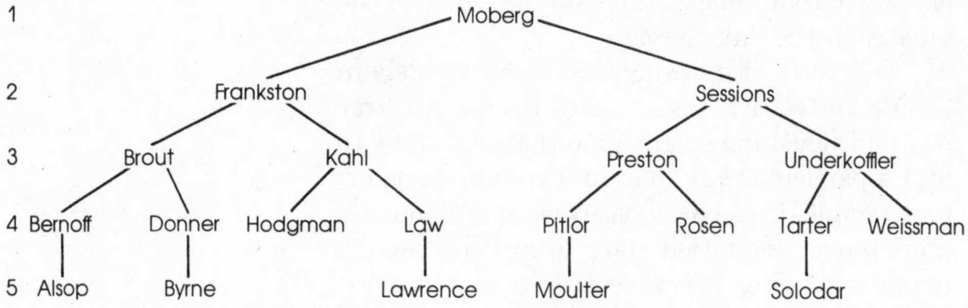

Figure 8-3: A B-tree with 20 Names

Procedural and Nonprocedural Software

You'll begin to hear more in the near future about procedural and nonprocedural DBMS programs. Most DBMS programs are strictly procedural (as is almost all software for the PC). Procedural programs require you to spell out each step in the solution to a problem. If the problem changes, a procedural program requires you to spell out the new way of solving it.

For example, look at the simple equation

$$AREA = LENGTH * WIDTH$$

If you don't know the WIDTH but do know the AREA and the LENGTH, procedural programs (like spreadsheets) or languages (like BASIC) demand that you redefine the problem, that is, tell the program exactly what to do. Nonprocedural programs rework the equation itself. The program can figure out that WIDTH = AREA/ LENGTH (or that MARGIN = GROSS PROFIT/REVENUE when you told the program only that REVENUE * MARGIN = GROSS PROFIT). There are few nonprocedural DBMS programs on the market at this time. They tend to be costly and to require large amounts of memory. What distinguishes them from procedural DBMS programs is that they claim to manipulate entire files rather than records.

The Taxonomy of DBMS Programs

DBMS programs fall into four general categories: file managers and relational, hierarchical, and network data base programs. Few programs are unadulterated versions of one or the other of those types. Among the DBMS programs available for microcomputers, most claim to be relational DBMS programs or file managers. However, most are also tinged with elements from hierarchical and network models.

Because DBMS programs are so much closer to being computer languages than spreadsheets or word processors are, it is difficult to discuss them in the absence of an application. So to keep this examination concrete, an example that many readers can relate to will be used—a magazine subscription. There's another reason for choosing a subscription data base. Most subscriptions are secured through direct-response marketing, and they have the same requirements as anything else marketed through the mail. A subscription system naturally involves list maintenance, with requirements similar to those faced by clubs, churches, alumni associations, and so forth. In short, a subscription example can be generalized more than some other examples.

File Managers

File managers are DBMS programs that are usually restricted to working with a single file at a time. If a file manager can use more than one file at a time, the files must be identically constructed. That is, each must have the same kinds of records and the same fields. For many simple applications, a file manager such as DBMaster or PFS:File is sufficient. The size of the application, by the way, isn't necessarily the key to whether a file manager is appropriate, because there are file managers that will massage more data than some sophisticated DBMS programs. The key is how frequently it is necessary to combine and recombine the data you keep.

Figure 8–4 is an example of how subscriber records might be kept in a file manager.

Code	Last	First	Address	City	St.	Zip	Expir.	Pd.
0987.781	Grescher	M.C.	25 Hill St	Harts Hill	NY	09877	07/85	Y
8460.020	Oelgeschlager	Margaret	2 Bishop's Gate Lane	Mission Viejo	CA	84601	01/86	N
9870.051	van Bowen	Jonathan	772 Thomas Ave	Walla Walla	WA	98702	10/85	Y

Figure 8-4: How Subscriber Records Might Be Kept in a File Manager

This figure shows a simple set of fields: it contains the information necessary to send a magazine to a subscriber (though it wouldn't come close to meeting the needs of a circulation manager at a real magazine). Notice that the file is kept in ascending zip code order. That fulfills a postal service requirement for zip-code-sorted mailings. Given those fields, you can print labels for a mailing, suspend subscribers who haven't paid, and send renewal notices when a subscription is about to lapse. But look at one of the problems involved in sending a renewal notice: because the records are in zip code order, they cannot be in date order by expiration date. To send renewal notices, you must select the records of subscribers whose expiration dates meet the criterion you set. That means that you also have to read all the records of those whose expiration dates do not meet the criterion.

One way around that is to re-sort the data base by expiration date, with the most imminent date at the beginning. Then you would have to read records only until you found the first that did not meet the criterion. Of course, you'd then have to re-sort the records you selected by zip codes in order to meet postal requirements, and you'd have to re-sort all the unselected records to return them to zip code order.

With 3 or 4—or even 100—records, that's no big deal. But as the records accumulate, all that sorting and re-sorting, and having to read records that do not meet the criterion, takes increasing amounts of time. That's especially true when you select records that are likely to constitute a minority of the records in the data base.

Let's complicate matters, as would be the case in a real subscription situation. Consider the other information you need to keep about a subscriber (or other kinds of customers): how was the subscription acquired in the first place? When was it first acquired? Was it paid by check, cash, or credit card? What kind of card and what's the card number and expiration date? Did the order come in with payment or did you send a bill? How often did you have to bill before you were paid? How many renewal notices were sent before you were paid? How much did this customer pay, and how many issues did the customer buy with that payment?

You would have to add a dozen more fields to the file. Doing that could reduce your flexibility rather than enhancing it. Each time you wished to do something with the data that you hadn't thought to do before, you might have to restructure the entire file. And every field you added would mean more data to examine unnecessarily.

If your reason for computerizing a filing system, which is all that a DBMS program does, is to allow you to organize and reorganize information to suit a variety of purposes, you will need a more flexible DBMS program than a file manager has to offer.

The Relational Model

In a relational DBMS program, all the information can be thought of as being set up in tabular files, similar to the one shown in figure 8-4. Each column of the table consists of fields, and each row in a table is a record. In fact, the file-manager example just explained could be called a relational file manager. A file manager is distinguished from a data base manager in that the latter can manipulate data that is contained in different files and use that data to create a new file.

Tip 72:

Relational Data Base versus File Manager

If you don't have logical subsets of your file(s), then you don't need a relational data base; you need a file manager. Don't use a Ferrari to drive to the drug store.

With a true DBMS program, you can deal with more than one file and the files can be structurally different. However, each record in each file contains a field that is found in another file. Those common fields are the points that relate one file to another. (Strictly speaking, the term *relational* is used because such data base programs are based on the mathematics of relational algebra and calculus.)

Why bother with so many different files? You've already seen one reason: to enable you to extract data without reading records unnecessarily. The more data you keep, the more data the program must examine if you ask it to select specific records. In the example above, when you want to send a renewal notice to all the subscribers whose subscription is due to lapse in July 1986, it's much easier to do so if you have a file organized by expiration date.

In larger list-maintenance applications, you can save a lot of file space and data-entry time if you keep a separate file of zip codes and the city and state to which they refer. Rather than including the city, state, and zip code in each customer's record, all you need is the zip code. When you have to mail something to the customer, you use the zip-code file to print the city and state on the mailing label.

Different DBMS programs have different limits on how many files you can keep open at one time; therefore, the number of files that can be used together efficiently differs, too. dBASE II permits you to keep open only two files at a time. In dBASE III, however, you can use up to ten files simultaneously. Four or five simultaneously open files is the practical maximum, however. Too many open files can lead to a great deal of confusion.

Keeping a file open means that its contents have been wholly or partially read and perhaps also written somewhere in the system—either in a buffer or a temporary scratch file on the disk—by the operating system or the program that's in control of the system. Changes that have been made to data in the file may also be somewhere in the system, but they have not yet been written to a file. The details will not be discussed here, but it's important to understand that at times files are created and used by the system without the intervention and beyond the control of the user. Also important are the implications of keeping multiple files open: you must have enough memory to support the program, the files it will use, and the overhead memory that managing open files demands.

The subscription file used above can be broken down into several files (see figure 8–5). One is an ACCOUNT file in which expiration dates and several other facts about the subscription are stored. Another is a ZIP-CODE file.

Tip 73:

Upgrading dBASE

Think twice before upgrading from dBASE II to dBASE III. Maybe only 5 percent of the code is substantially different, but the changes are crucial. Updating major applications could be quite costly.

Tip 74:

The Memory Hog

DBMS software uses a lot of memory. It also reads and writes files to the disk often, some files that you are aware of and many that you never see. For that reason, if you use DBMS programs you should probably have a hard disk. Read and write access is much faster, for one thing. For another, data bases tend to consume far more space than you would imagine, and you will soon tire of playing swap-the-floppy.

Tip 75:

File Structure

If you are using a true DBMS program, not a file manager, then there really shouldn't be a need to sort it often. If you are doing a lot of sorting, think about restructuring the files. That may seem like a lot of work, but it will pay off eventually.

The SUBSCRIBER file contains only codes, names, street addresses, and a zip code. A SUSPEND file has been added to handle subscriptions that have not been paid (billed but unpaid, bad credit card, etc.), that have been returned because of a bad address, or that for some other reason are not being fulfilled. Another file could also have been created for expired subscriptions. This system is still a long way from fulfilling the needs of a real subscription manager, but it is much more complex than the earlier version for use with the file manager.

Notice that each file contains a field that can be used as the entry to another file. The code-number field in the ACCOUNT file is the connection with the name-and-address file, and

ACCOUNT File

Expir	Code	Pmt	Sc	Pd	Type
07/85	0987.781	9.95	01	1	0
10/85	8460.020	9.95	08	1	1
01/86	9870.051	11.00	97	0	3

ZIP CODE File

Zip	City	
09877	Harts Hill	NY
84601	Mission Viejo	CA
98702	Walla Walla	WA

SUBSCRIBER File

Code	Last	First	Address	Zip
0987.781	Grescher	M.C.	25 Hill St	84601
8460.020	van Bowen	Jonathan	772 Thomas Ave	98702
9870.051	Oelgeschlager	Margaret	2 Bishop's Gate Lane	09877

SUSPEND File

Code	Rsn
0987.781	00
8477.020	06
9165.051	12

Figure 8-5: A More Complex Subscription File

the zip-code field in the name-and-address file is the connection with the zip-code file. A field in a record that connects that record to another file is called a *foreign key*. A field that is used as the organizing item in the record itself is called a *primary key*.

When the time comes that you need all the information in all the files combined into a single large file you invoke the JOIN command.

The reasons for locking the data base are varied. One obvious reason is to protect confidential information, such as financial records, a patient's records, your list of prospective customers, and so forth. That's one kind of locking, but there's another important kind: concurrent-use locking. Imagine two airline reservation agents selling the same seat. When the first agent opens a file to see which seats are available, the second agent should not be able to write to the file until the first agent is finished updating it.

Concurrent-use locking implies unlocking, and it should not be left to the user to unlock after use, because people sometimes forget such things, leaving other users in the cold. One of the problems to think about if you are locking a data base against concurrent use is to prevent deadlocks. If data base users can share files and if multiple files can be open at the same time, there will be times when user 1 opens file A for updating while user 2 holds file B open for updating. If user 2 then calls for file A and is locked out, he should not be placed in "wait" mode until file A is open again. That's because user 1 might call file B and wind up in the same position, waiting for the file to be freed. Because user 1 can't go back to file A until file B is open and user 2 can't go back to file B until A is open, the two users will circle the landing field forever.

Some information about a customer will rarely or perhaps never change: the source of

Locking

Tip 76:

More Overhead Than You Think

We've said that data bases are memory consumers. Even a small data base uses a lot of space. What are you really talking about when you discuss a data base's size? Imagine a data base with fields that need 300 characters. (A name, address, zip code, and telephone number alone will equal 150 characters.) If you have only 650 records in that data base, you have a potential of 195,000 characters, not including the characters necessary to identify fields, ends of records, pointers, keys, and so forth.

the business (where you first got it—in sales it's the source of the lead, in direct marketing the magazine, mailing, and so forth from which the first order was placed); the density, tensile strength, and elasticity of materials; the date the customer placed his first order, and so on. Don't clutter up a file that needs a lot of updating with fields that never change; Put them in separate files.

Normalization

Once you have been using data base software for a while, you'll encounter questions of *normalization.* The term refers to a set of five rules dealing with how you construct the files used in a relational data base. Called the first normal form (1NF), the second normal form (2NF), and so on, the normalization rules are not laws but guidelines for designing a data base application. Ignoring them doesn't mean that you will suffer dire consequences, such as losing your data, but it may mean that you create an application that is less than completely efficient. You may find, for example, that it is easy to get your data into the system but much harder to get it out, or that combining files isn't as easy as you thought.

The first normal form specifies that a field may contain only one value; the second normal form specifies that each nonkey field must be a single fact about the (entire) key. According to the third normal form, a nonkey field should not contain a fact about another nonkey field, and according to the fourth normal form, one-to-many relationships should be represented by a foreign key in the "many" table that matches the primary key in the "one" table. Finally, the fifth normal form specifies that, for many-to-many relationships, you should use a separate table consisting of foreign keys that together make up the primary key for the table.

The Hierarchical Model

The hierarchical DBMS program is more complicated than the relational one. Relationships between units of information are indicated by the use of *pointers*. In Jonathan van Bowen's case, for example, his name would be in one field. Associated with that field would be the address of another field in which his expiration date is located and another in which his code number is located. Each field may point to, or contain the address of, one or more other fields. If a field contains no information, the address pointer is left blank and no space is used for the field. Records may be of different sizes, which is helpful if someone has two addresses. Traditionally, fields that point to other fields are called *parents,* and the fields that are pointed to are called *children*. A child may have only one parent, but a parent may have more than one child. Another common analogy is that of the tree, with the first field being the *root* of the tree and the subsequent levels being the *branches*.

One advantage of a hierarchical structure is that there is no unused, and thereby wasted, space. A disadvantage is the fact that it is difficult and time-consuming to change the data base structure once it is established.

In a hierarchical data base, the sample information used in the subscription example could look like figure 8–6. Suppose M. C. Grescher wrote in and said that she wanted the bill for her subscription to be sent to her home but

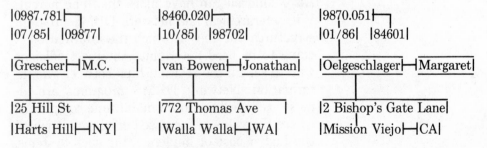

Figure 8-6: Hierarchical Data Base Structure

that the magazine itself should be sent to her office. If this were a relational data base, a second record for Ms. Grescher would have to be added. That could create problems at renewal time if a notice were sent to every record showing the same expiration date. Should Ms. Grescher be billed twice because she has two addresses? And how do you deal with her bill if she pays it and is credited at the wrong address?

There would be no problem representing this in a hierarchical data base. There would only be one record for Ms. Grescher (see figure 8-7).

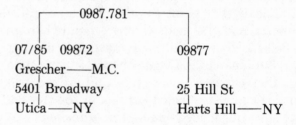

Figure 8-7: A Record with Two Addresses in a Hierarchical Data Base

The Network Model

A network DBMS program, sometimes called the Codasyl model (after the Conference on Data Systems Languages), is the most complex of the DBMS structures. Like a hierarchical DBMS program, a network DBMS program uses pointers. The major difference is that if one field in a network data base points to a second, the second field can point back to the first one. Also, children can have more than one parent. With hierarchical and network DBMS program structures, the way in which the information is going to be used determines the most efficient way to set up the relationships between the information. Network DBMS programs are almost exclusively used on mainframe computers, where the value of increased efficiency is worth the higher cost of implementing such systems.

In the sample subscriber data base, there

might be two subscribers at the same address. The hierarchical structure wouldn't be able to represent that situation easily, because a child (in this case the address) can have only one parent (name of the subscriber). However, because a network model allows children to have more than one parent, the data could be structured as shown in figure 8–8.

```
   ┌─0987.781           ┌─0987.661─┐
  07/85  09872          06/86    09872
  Grescher──M.C.       Peterson,──John A.
   └──────5401 Broadway─┘
               Utica──NY
```

Figure 8-8: Network Model Structure

Ending the book with a tip about realistic expectations may be contrary to what many salespeople will tell you. The microcomputer will not solve all your business problems, but it can make your work flow more smoothly and rapidly if you take the time to examine software and hardware before you make a purchase, and if you then allow yourself time to learn. When your planning is well thought out, then you're likely to state (paraphrasing Tip #55), "Microcomputers have changed my life."

The Boston Computer Society hopes that *Things the Manual Never Told You* has made your work with the IBM PC a bit easier and that this book will continue to be a useful reference for you.

Tip 77:

Realistic Expectations

If you have a mainframe background, don't expect too much. If it's on a PC, it'll be slow. A micro data base, in speed, compares with the slowest of high-level languages—COBOL.

Index